"In Case Atom Bombs Fall"

ALSO BY MICHAEL SCHEIBACH

*Atomic Narratives and American Youth:
Coming of Age with the Atom, 1945–1955*
(McFarland, 2003)

"In Case Atom Bombs Fall"

An Anthology of Governmental Explanations, Instructions and Warnings from the 1940s to the 1960s

Edited by
MICHAEL SCHEIBACH

McFarland & Company, Inc., Publishers
Jefferson, North Carolina, and London

LIBRARY OF CONGRESS CATALOGUING-IN-PUBLICATION DATA

"In case atom bombs fall" : an anthology of governmental explanations, instructions and warnings from the 1940s to the 1960s / edited by Michael Scheibach.
p.   cm.

Includes bibliographical references and index.

ISBN 978-0-7864-4541-7
softcover : 50# alkaline paper ∞

1. Civil defense — United States — History — 20th century — Sources.
2. Nuclear warfare — Social aspects — United States.
3. Cold War — Social aspects — United States.
I. Scheibach, Michael, 1949–

UA927.I5   2009   363.350973'09045 — dc22   2009025965

British Library cataloguing data are available

©2009 Michael Scheibach. All rights reserved

No part of this book may be reproduced or transmitted in any form or by any means, electronic or mechanical, including photocopying or recording, or by any information storage and retrieval system, without permission in writing from the publisher.

On the cover: main image *Survival Under Atomic Attack*, 1950 (National Security Resources Board, Civil Defense Office); three insets *Just in Case Atom Bombs Fall*, 1951 (Civil Defense Office of Denver)

Manufactured in the United States of America

McFarland & Company, Inc., Publishers
Box 611, Jefferson, North Carolina 28640
www.mcfarlandpub.com

For Archer, Scarlett, and my future grandchildren.
May they and their generation grow up in a world at peace.

Table of Contents

Introduction	1
Prologue: This Is Civil Defense	7

Part 1 — The A-Bomb

Hiroshima	13
Atomic Basics	16
Operation Crossroads	19
Understanding the Atomic Bomb	25
Six Survival Secrets for Atomic Attacks	30

Part 2 — Radioactive Fallout

From "Initial" to "Lingering" Fallout	33
Facts About Fallout	38
Nuclear Fallout	39
Radioactivity Is Nothing New	45
Fallout on the Farm	46

Part 3 — Women and the Home

The Bomb and the Baby	53
Women in Civil Defense	55
At Home!! Are You Prepared	60
Grandma's Pantry	61
Home Defense Corps	65
Home Defense Can Help You Prepare Now	68
Medical Aides	69

Part 4 — Be Prepared

Home Defense Pledge	75
Operation Alert	76
CONELRAD	83
If You Have Had No Warning in an A-Bomb Attack	86
Look to the Sky	88
Plane Spotters	92
What to Do If You're Bombed	94
Before and During an Atomic Attack	100
Facts About the H Bomb	105
Don't Panic	108
3 Minutes of Your Time	111
Common Sense	113

Part 5 — Duck and Cover

"Atomics" in Education	119
Atomic Activities	129
The National Defense Pattern	133
Prepare for the Worst	134
School Shelters	140

Part 6 — Find Shelter

Survival Requirements	147
Shelter Supplies	150
Shelter from Fallout	153
Shelter Preparation	158
Before Disaster Strikes	162
Know How to Survive	164
If an Attack Occurs	167

Part 7 — Evacuate

Highways for Civil Defense	171
Evacuation Guide	175
Will to Survive	177
Value of Shelters	180
Survival of the Fittest	181
Evacuation Rules and Routes	186
4 Wheels to Survival	191
Don't Be There	192

PART 8—PEACE ... OR ELSE

It Could Happen Here!	198
"Atoms for Peace"	199
Nuclear Test Ban Treaty	206
Postscript: First Steps Toward Recovery	212
Save This Book	214
Bibliography of Civil Defense Publications, 1950–1965	215
Index	217

Introduction

Americans welcomed the news with celebratory joy and quiet relief. The war, proclaimed President Harry S Truman, had come to an end with receipt of Emperor Hirohito's unconditional surrender. What began on Sunday morning, December 7, 1941, with a Japanese attack on Pearl Harbor, a little-known naval base somewhere in the Pacific Ocean, concluded on Tuesday evening, August 14, 1945, eight days after a specially equipped B-29 Superfortress dropped a new weapon — an atomic bomb — on the Japanese city of Hiroshima. The bomb killed 70,000 people instantly, many completely vaporized from the heat of the blast, which reached 5400 degrees Fahrenheit at ground zero.

In a statement released the day after the annihilation of Hiroshima, President Truman told the country that Japan had been "repaid many fold" for its unprovoked assault on Pearl Harbor. He also stressed the necessity of the United States to guard the secrets of the atomic bomb in order to protect "us and the rest of the world from the danger of sudden destruction." The Atomic Age — with all its repercussions — had begun.

Shortly after the U.S. dropped a second atomic bomb on Nagasaki — three days following Hiroshima — *Time* magazine proclaimed this all-powerful force had given civilization a "brutal challenge" to save itself from destruction. Noted journalist and editor Norman Cousins wrote in the August 18 issue of *Saturday Review of Literature*, "Whatever elation there is in the world today because of final victory in the war is severely tempered by fear." Yet for a country exhausted by war, welcoming home GIs, rekindling family ties, and retooling the economy from war production to consumer goods took precedence. Even though the atomic bomb had, most Americans acknowledged, escalated the potential of an eventual Armageddon, the fact remained that the United States had a monopoly over the bomb, at least for now.

During the late 1940s, government and scientific rhetoric remained focused on the unlimited potential and apocalyptic power of the atom. On the one hand, the atom promised breakthroughs in such areas as energy and medicine; on the other hand, the atom threatened to destroy civilization if a third world war — an atomic war — were to occur. The catch phrases during this period were "one world or none" and "peace ... or else."

Historian William Graebner has called the late 1940s the "age of doubt," resulting in large part from the uncertainties and trepidations revolving around the atomic bomb, especially the potential of the Soviet Union becoming an atomic power. Congress confronted the country's concerns with passage of the National Security Act of 1947, which created the National Security Resources Board and its Civil Defense Office. Within two years, however, what had been a future possibility became a stark reality with the Soviet

Union's successful test of its own atomic bomb in September 1949. The Atomic Age, which had begun just four years earlier, became even more threatening as the Cold War solidified into two major adversarial powers. The monopoly had ended, and the federal government had to make sure all Americans not only understood the new Soviet threat, but also had the requisite knowledge and skills to survive an atomic attack and, perhaps more important, the ability and commitment to ensure the country's future in the aftermath of atomic destruction.

Congress again acted by passing the Federal Civil Defense Act in 1950. The following year, President Truman created the Federal Civil Defense Administration, which immediately began disseminating information about the nature of the atom, descriptions of the effects of an atomic blast, instructions for surviving an atomic bomb, and warnings about the potential destructive power of an atomic attack on American cities.

The present work provides a sampling of publications issued by federal, state, and local government agencies and civil defense organizations between 1950 and the early 1960s. These publications span the country, from New York to Oregon, Alabama to Wisconsin. Illustrations featured on the following pages offer a visual glimpse of both the serious and humorous sides of civil defense; and the original punctuation and typographic styles (e.g., **boldface**, *italic*, and ALL CAP text) are used to maintain the emphasis placed on specific warnings and instructions. Some of the publications are one- or two-page brochures or posters that are best reproduced as full-page facsimiles, rather than as text. In the table of contents, an italicized title denotes such cases. Editorial notes in italics precede each piece, and provide some specific background and context. The book is arranged thematically, with sections covering the impact and power of the atomic bomb, radioactive fallout, women and the home, the importance of being prepared, civil defense in schools, fallout shelters, evacuation plans, and, finally, the call for "peace or ... else."

These civil defense publications offer a unique insight into the government's well-organized efforts to inform, educate, and prepare all Americans for the potentiality of nuclear war. At the same time, they also reveal contemporary social attitudes, particularly relating to women and the family. For example, car pools were encouraged not to save gas, but rather to ensure that family members at home had an automobile available to evacuate if the warning signals sounded. The car represented "four wheels to survival." Publications reminded women to keep their homes and yards clean of debris in order to minimize fires resulting from an atomic blast, and to stock foods and emergency supplies for their home fallout shelters. As one pamphlet said, "The home is the basic unit of the community — and the basic unit on which defense of the home front must be built. Whether you are a housewife, secretary, business executive, or nurse, civil defense looks to you, as a woman, to take an active role in protecting your home. No one else can do that job for you.... Getting America prepared on the home front is a responsibility that falls in large part on the shoulders of all American women."

Women answered the call by becoming front-line workers in civil defense organizations, such as the Home Defense Corps in Milwaukee and certified Medical Aides in the State of New York. Local civil defense offices distributed identification tags; parents and children alike memorized warning signals; and families practiced driving on evacuation routes, sometimes 50 miles each way. Schools incorporated atomic themes in classroom curricula, conducted surprise duck-and-cover drills, provided well-stocked shelters within their facilities, and assumed responsibility for protecting children in case of a surprise attack during school hours. America's youths did their part by becoming "plane spotters" in the Ground Observer Corps, which at its peak had 800,000 civilian volunteers watching the skies for enemy aircraft approaching America's cities.

Civil defense became a citizen's patriotic duty. "Across the nation," said a 1953 brochure, "great numbers of men and women have already joined Civil Defense. They are training and participating in test exercises, manning the Civil Defense services that will work together to save lives and restore our cities after an atomic attack."

By the mid–1950s, both the United States and the Soviet Union possessed hydrogen bombs — packing the explosive power of millions of tons of TNT, compared to just 20,000 tons of TNT in the Hiroshima bomb, and extending the deadly reach of radioactive fallout. Allan Winkler, in *Life Under a Cloud: American Anxiety About the Atom*, argues that most Americans "wondered whether anyone, anywhere in the world, could withstand the invisible consequences of a nuclear attack. Had they created a Frankenstein monster that would kill them in silent, insidious ways? Were they fiddling with the future of the human race by developing bigger and better bombs? Those questions dominated public debate in the second decade of the atomic age."

The massive escalation in nuclear capability, coupled with an equal escalation in people's fears, prompted the government to release its National Policy on Shelters in 1958, outlining plans for identifying existing structures to serve as fallout shelters, as well as for encouraging the construction of personal and community shelters. According to the new policy, described in Part 6, all Americans had a responsibility for civil defense. "Protection of our people is not new in the United States," stated Leo A. Hoegh, director of the Office of Civil and Defense Mobilization in 1958. "When a free America was being built by our forebears, every log cabin and every dwelling had a dual purpose — namely, a home and a fortress. Today, the citizen should be called upon to make the same contribution as our forebears — not for building a free America, but for sustaining a free America."

In addition to government-sponsored publications, *"In Case Atom Bombs Fall"* includes statements from the three presidents during this period: Harry S Truman, Dwight D. Eisenhower, and John F. Kennedy. President Truman's initial statement following the 1945 bombing of Hiroshima warned the Japanese that if they did not surrender immediately, "they may expect a rain of ruin from the air, the like of which has never been seen on this earth." President Eisenhower's address before the United Nations in 1953 promoted "Atoms for Peace," which lead to an international program that supplied equipment and information to schools, hospitals, and other institutions. And President Kennedy's call in 1963 for a ban on nuclear testing eventually led to the Partial Test Ban Treaty, which banned nuclear tests in the atmosphere, under water, and in outer space.

A radio transcript from an August 7, 1945, broadcast on station WIP in Philadelphia, provides one of the first scientific explanations of the "new" atomic bomb, by Dr. Roy K. Marshall, director of the Fels Planetarium of The Franklin Institute. The official report on the 1946 atomic tests in the Bikini Islands, located 2,000 miles southwest of Hawaii, summarizes the preliminary results of two atomic detonations, one an air burst and the other exploded under water. The tests occurred in a lagoon containing 90 older battleships, aircraft carriers, destroyers, heavy cruisers, submarines, and assorted smaller vessels, with some 42,000 men, 37,000 of them Navy personnel, present as observers. An excerpt from the study that led to the National Interstate and Defense Highways Act of 1956 is included for its prominent place in the history of the Atomic Age. The Act, signed into law by President Eisenhower, provided $25 billion to construct 41,000 miles of interstate highways — not simply to improve transportation, as the study reveals, but also to expedite the evacuation of people from "target" cities.

Operation Alert, held each year between 1954 and 1961, tested the government's ability to respond to an enemy attack. Operation Alert began with hypothetical nuclear bombs exploding in Washington, D.C., and scores of cities throughout the country, and included thousands of government and military personnel, as well as citizen volunteers. Local civil defense planning, communication systems, transportation centers, warning alerts, and responses to fallout were among the areas tested. In April 1958, Innis D. Harris, an evaluation officer for the 1957 test, presented his findings before members of the Industrial College of Armed Forces. His comments, included in Part 4, offer a historical background to Operation Alert and a candid analysis of the government's performance.

Today, more than a half century separates us from those years of mock nuclear attacks, surprise drills, fallout shelters, warning signs on buses and in office buildings, and television images of atomic bombs exploding in the Nevada desert. Looking back from our 21st-century vantage point, we still grimace at the descriptions of impending death and destruction, and yet we can laugh at the hyperbolic prose and humorous illustrations related to surviving an atomic attack. It's important, however, that we not forget that concerns about "weapons of mass destruction" originated in the late 1940s. Nor should we dismiss the fact that Americans living in the formative years of the Cold War — from 1945 through the early 1960s — believed the threat of a nuclear war was very real indeed. Even more significant, they understood quite clearly that their lives could end at any moment in a blinding flash. During these years, all Americans — young and old, male and female, urban and rural — confronted the realities of "The Bomb" everywhere they ventured: at work, at home, in their communities, and at school.

President Kennedy proved prophetic in his 1963 call for a treaty to ban nuclear tests when he said, "I ask you to stop and think for a moment what it would mean to have nuclear weapons in so many hands, in the hands of countries large and small, stable and unstable, responsible and irresponsible, scattered throughout the world. There would be no rest for anyone then, no stability, no real security, and no chance of effective disarmament. There would only be the increased chance of accidental war, and an increased necessity for the great powers to involve themselves in what otherwise would be local conflicts."

Although the Cold War has officially ended, and the Soviet Union irreparably splintered, the United States still faces an atomic threat of a more elusive nature — potentially arising from a terrorist organization or a rogue nation. For this reason, the explanations, instructions, advice, and dire warnings that follow may once again become relevant and worthy of a second look.

TO THE READER:

- This booklet is prepared to help you in case of an atomic bomb attack.
- Read this **now** — before anything happens.
- Be sure the other members of your family know what to do.
- You may have no warning other than a flash of light.

- Pick out in advance the best shelter nearest your home, your place of work or church. This would be in a cellar, or behind walls, or even behind a pile of dirt.
- Find out **now** how to shut off gas, water and electricity where the pipes have entered the house, and label the shut-offs.
- Find out how to contact the local Civil Defense in case you need aid or instruction.

From *Protection from the Atomic Bomb*, Civil Defense Agency of the Commonwealth of Massachusetts, 1950.

Prologue: This Is Civil Defense

Modern civil defense is nothing like civil defense in previous wars. Where once our danger was from fire bombs and high explosives, now it is from atomic, biological, and new chemical weapons. The wide oceans that used to protect us have given way to the global bomber. Today we face more kinds of attack than ever before, and our danger is much greater.

This booklet was written to give you, as a responsible American citizen, the straight facts on why civil defense is needed, how it works, and what part you must play to make it a success.

What Is Civil Defense?

Civil defense is a way of saving lives and property. It is a way of protecting you and your family in case of war on the United States. It is a way of helping to keep you going, and to keep production going, in spite of atomic, biological, or chemical attacks.

One of the chief aims of civil defense is to help you to stay at work no matter what may come. Unless all of us kept at our jobs in the face of attack, the enemy would win the war. His aim would be to make you and others quit — desert your cities so that our defense plants would shut down. *Your* aim would be to keep working and to give our armed forces the things they need to beat the enemy.

Can America Be Attacked?

Yes. At any time.

Right now enemy planes can reach every major city in the United States. We know that Russia has heavy, long-range bombers patterned after our own B-29. Most of these bombers could get through our defenses if an attack came.... President Truman has said we must assume Russia has atomic bombs. We know there has been an atomic explosion in Russia.

Can We Defend Ourselves?

There is no known way of preventing most enemy bombers from reaching their targets in the United States.

Gen. Hoyt Vandenberg, Chief of Staff of the United States Air Force, has said that *at most* we could knock down only 30 out of each 100 enemy planes attacking the United States. At least 7 out of 10 would get through....

You can be sure that everything possible will be done to stop the enemy at our borders, and to stop sabotage before it starts within our borders. But you also can be sure that, in case of war, a good percentage of enemy attacks would be successful in spite of all we could do.

That is why we must have civil defense — and have it now!

What Would Happen If an Atomic Bomb Fell on Your City?

Imagine even one atomic bomb being dropped on an American city — your city, for example. Many thousands of persons would be killed instantly. Many thousands of others would be wounded and in need of immediate care. Many hundreds more would be trapped or buried in the wreckage. Every street within the major damage area would be completely blocked with rubble. Fires would start within a matter of minutes in many places at once.

These are the main things that could happen, but there are others. For instance, a large part of the city's food supply might be destroyed or cut off. The water supply might be knocked out. Regular communications might stop entirely. Much of the transportation system certainly would stop. Thousands of survivors would suddenly find themselves homeless, without food, clothing, shelter, or money.

Most Americans in the 1950s could instantly recognize images of Lucy, Howdy Doody, Superman, and, most important, the civil defense symbol. Whether at work or at school, watching television or out for a Sunday afternoon drive, Americans of all ages understood the meaning behind this symbol.

What Could Happen Without Civil Defense?

Ask the Japanese.

Hiroshima and Nagasaki had almost no civil defense as we know it. When atomic bombs were dropped, their citizens were almost completely unprepared. Result: The people panicked badly. Many thousands were needlessly hurt or killed, families were broken up, property was lost. Thousands were left homeless with no one to care for them. The wounded and helpless, who might otherwise have lived, died because proper civil defense was not organized to save them.

But there was something of even greater importance to a nation that was fighting for its life. The fact that there was no civil defense meant that the factories left standing after the atomic blast could not operate.

Without civil defense a nation is helpless. With it, cities can get up off the floor and fight back after an attack. Casualties can be cut in half.

What Are the Biggest Civil Defense Problems?

Public education, training, and organization.

We need civil defense training immediately for some 15,000,000 Americans, and intensive education in self-protection for 135,000,000 more. The most staggering civil defense problem is the size of the training and organization jobs to be done.

Try to picture the number of trained workers that would be needed to handle an attack situation. As an example, a single first-aid station should consist of almost 200 workers. They could handle about 600 wounded people in 24 hours.

Nearly 100 such first-aid stations would be needed to care for those injured by one Hiroshima-size atomic bomb. So, more than 20,000 first-aid workers would be needed for each atomic bomb, and this doesn't include hospital staffs.

Before first-aiders could reach the wounded, an engineering service as large or even larger would be needed to clear the rubble. A highly trained rescue service would be needed to get people out of wrecked or burning buildings. A large and efficient supply service would be needed to bring in food, clothing, and medicine. There would be other jobs of putting out fires, restoring utilities, caring for the homeless, gathering families together again, feeding the people, and getting the factories and community life rolling once more.

Most of the ways of meeting atomic disaster are not new or different, except in size. The biggest problem is to prepare ourselves to handle catastrophes greater than any that ever have struck the United States. The problem can be met only through civil defense. Each of us must have a job to do if trouble comes—*and must know how to do it.*

This Is Civil Defense
Federal Civil Defense Administration, 1951

Part 1
The A-Bomb

Photograph of the atomic bombing of Hiroshima, August 6, 1945 (National Archives).

Hiroshima

At 8:15 A.M. (Japanese time) on Monday, August 6, 1945, a specially equipped American B-29 Superfortress dropped the first atomic bomb on the city of Hiroshima. The bomb killed an estimated 70,000 people instantly and vaporized everything at ground zero. Thousands more died later from blast-related injuries and radiation poisoning. The attack occurred Sunday evening in the United States. The next day, President Harry S Truman issued the following statement to the American people.

Sixteen hours ago, an American airplane dropped one bomb on Hiroshima and destroyed its usefulness to the enemy. That bomb had more power than 20,000 tons of T.N.T. It had more than two thousand times the blast power of the British "Grand Slam," which is the largest bomb ever yet used in the history of warfare.

The Japanese began the war from the air at Pearl Harbor. They have been repaid many fold. And the end is not yet. With this bomb, we have now added a new and revolutionary increase in destruction to supplement the growing power of our armed forces. In their present form, these bombs are now in production and even more powerful forms are in development.

It is an atomic bomb. It is a harnessing of the basic power of the universe. The force from which the sun draws its power has been loosed against those who brought war to the Far East.

Before 1939, it was the accepted belief of scientists that it was theoretically possible to release atomic energy. But no one knew any practical method of doing it. By 1942, however, we knew that the Germans were working feverishly to find a way to add atomic energy to the other engines of war with which they hoped to enslave the world. But they failed. We may be grateful to Providence that the Germans got the V-1's and V-2's late and in limited quantities and even more grateful that they did not get the atomic bomb at all.

The battle of the laboratories held fateful risks for us as well as the battles of the air, land and sea, and we have now won the battle of the laboratories as we have won the other battles.

Beginning in 1940, before Pearl Harbor, scientific knowledge useful in war was pooled between the United States and Great Britain, and many priceless helps to our victories have come from that arrangement. Under that general policy, the research on the atomic bomb was begun. With American and British scientists working together, we entered the race of discovery against the Germans.

The United States had available the large number of scientists of distinction in the many needed areas of knowledge. It had the tremendous industrial and financial resources necessary for the project and they could be devoted to it without undue impairment of other vital war work. In the United States, the laboratory work and the production plans, on which a substantial start had already been made, would be out of reach of enemy bombing, while at that time Britain was exposed to constant air attack and was still threatened with the possibility of invasion. For these reasons, Prime Minister Churchill and President Roosevelt agreed that it was wise to carry on the project here. We now have two great plans and many lesser works devoted to the production of atomic power. Employment during peak construction numbered 125,000 and over 65,000 individuals are even now engaged in operating the plants. Many have worked there for two and a half years. Few know what they have been producing. They see great quantities of material going in and they see nothing coming out of these plants, for the physical size of the explosive charge is exceedingly small. We have spent two billion dollars on the greatest scientific gamble in history — and won.

But the greatest marvel is not the size of the enterprise, its secrecy, nor its cost, but the achievement of scientific brains in putting together infinitely complex pieces of knowledge held by many men in different fields of science into a workable plan. And hardly less marvelous has been the capacity of industry to design, and of labor to operate, the machines and methods to do things never done before so that the brain child of many minds came forth in physical shape and performed as it was supposed to do. Both science and industry worked under the direction of the United States Army, which achieved a unique success in managing so diverse a problem in the advancement of knowledge in an amazingly short time. It is doubtful if such another combination could be got together in the world. What has been done is the greatest achievement of organized science in history. It was done under high pressure and without failure.

We are now prepared to obliterate more rapidly and completely every productive enterprise the Japanese have above ground in any city. We shall destroy their docks, their factories, and their communications. Let there be no mistake; we shall completely destroy Japan's power to make war.

It was to spare the Japanese people from utter destruction that the ultimatum of July 26 was issued at Potsdam. Their leaders promptly rejected that ultimatum. If they do not now accept our terms, they may expect a rain of ruin from the air, the like of which has never been seen on this earth. Behind this air attack will follow sea and land forces in such numbers and power as they have not yet seen and with the fighting skill of which they are already well aware.

The Secretary of War, who has kept in personal touch with all phases of the project, will immediately make public a statement giving further details.

His statement will give facts concerning the sites at Oak Ridge near Knoxville, Tennessee, and at Richland near Pasco, Washington, and an installation near Santa Fe, New Mexico. Although the workers at the sites have been making materials to be used in producing the greatest destructive force in history, they have not themselves been in danger beyond that of many other occupations, for the utmost care has been taken of their safety.

The fact that we can release atomic energy ushers in a new era in man's understanding of nature's forces. Atomic energy may in the future supplement the power that now comes from coal, oil, and falling water, but at present it cannot be produced on a basis to compete with them commercially. Before that comes there must be a long period of intensive research.

It has never been the habit of scientists of this country or the policy of this Government to withhold from the world scientific knowledge. Normally, therefore, everything about the work with atomic energy would be made public.

But under present circumstances, it is not intended to divulge the technical processes of production or all the military applications, pending further examination of possible methods of protecting us and the rest of the world from the danger of sudden destruction.

I shall recommend that the Congress of the United States consider promptly the establishment of an appropriate commission to control the production and use of atomic power within the United States. I shall give further consideration and make further recommendations to the Congress as to how atomic power can become a powerful and forceful influence towards the maintenance of world peace.

Atomic Basics

Radio station WIP in Philadelphia, owned at the time by the now defunct Gimbel Broadcasting System, moved quickly to explain this new destructive weapon—and new form of energy—that exploded without warning on August 6, 1945. The day after the bombing of Hiroshima, Dr. Roy K. Marshall, director of the Fels Planetarium of The Franklin Institute, broadcast the following presentation, titled "Atomic Bomb," which explained the basics of atomic energy and the atomic bomb from a scientist's perspective.

Most of you, in hearing the news during the last few hours—news about this new weapon of destruction that has been loosed on the world and, fortunately, on our enemies and not on ourselves—have dreamed a little about the things you have read in amazing magazine stories of the past; this thing couldn't quite be real. It is, nevertheless, quite real and certainly, at least on the part of the scientists, it was to be expected. That is, the release of the energy, the power, from the hearts of atoms has not come to the scientific world in general as anything of a surprise. That it has been released first as a weapon of war is, of course, something we could not anticipate many years ago when the work began.

We've got to think for a moment of one statement made by President Truman when the release of the bomb was announced, to explain why I'm here. Astronomers are not always the fellows who lie beneath great telescopes and look into the sky counting the stars. We sometimes wonder about the stars, what they are and where they get their energy; in the course of that wondering we made up our minds long ago—more than forty years ago—that the stars certainly could not be burning because any efficient method of burning that we know here on Earth would imply that the stars would last a very short time. To render that a little more concrete, I should say this: If the sun were composed entirely of coal—the very finest coal imaginable—and if we could set it afire and burn it as efficiently as we know how, the sun would last only about 5,000 years. And yet we know that the sun has been shining with undiminished energy and certainly no conspicuous change of energy output for at least the past two billion years. The Earth's crust has been essentially as we know it today for the past two thousand million years, and that means that the sun has been shining with the same energy output and by the same mechanism for at least that long. It would be very strange, indeed, if after as short a time as 5,000 years in the future, the sun should cease to shine. Therefore, on the basis of common sense—and astronomers do have that once in a while—we could conclude that burning is not the source of the sun's energy.

What, then, could it possibly be? Well, at about the time these speculations were beginning to be expressed and questions about them were being asked and the answers from a common-sense standpoint were being given, the physicists and chemists in their laboratories were beginning to learn more about atoms; and little by little, they gradually realized that in the atom there was a source of power which, if tapped, would surpass anything we could possibly imagine as a fuel.

Now we understand a little about what an atom is. An atom is the smallest unit of a chemical element. That is, if you hold a chunk of gold in your hand—pure gold, no alloy, no impurity—you must realize that the gold consists of atoms. Each atom consists of a nucleus which contains almost all of the mass of the atom and around that nucleus there revolve little particles, with negative electrical charges, that we call electrons. They are going around the nucleus as the planets go around the sun. And now that I have introduced the electrons—the little negative charges—forget about them! We're interested in the core, the heart, the nucleus of the atom. The nucleus consists of two different kinds of particles—positively charged particles called protons and particles with no electrical charge, called neutrons. You see, they are electrically neutral, so we call them neutrons; the positively charged particles are protons.

Now, if you mix protons and neutrons in a certain proportion, what you have is the nucleus of an atom of gold. If you choose other numbers and other proportions of them, you may have an atom of chlorine gas. If you mix them in other amounts, you may have some other element, such as uranium. If you have a lot of protons and neutrons—92 protons and 146 neutrons—you have ordinary uranium that is called U-238 because there are 238 particles in the nucleus. If you have a different mixture—92 protons and 143 neutrons—you have what is called U-235 because of the 235 particles in the nucleus. It is still uranium, however, because there are 92 protons, and uranium is number 92 in the complete table of the chemical elements.

I have arrived at U-235 in a hurry because that is probably the source of the power we are now getting from the atom, for use in the atomic bomb. That has been no secret, except in the sense that we don't know where we are getting enough U-235, and certainly if I knew I wouldn't tell you. We know that U-235 can be used and it probably is being used....

At the time of the outbreak of the war, there was no way to manufacture U-235 commercially—for, to get any considerable quantity of it, it must be manufactured. There isn't enough of it in the earth easily obtainable; we must begin with other materials—such as other ordinary forms of uranium—and build atoms of U-235. In building these, we use energy obtained in ordinary ways, but the amount is less by far than the amount of energy we get from the destruction of atoms of U-235. The resulting amount of energy surpasses anything that even I, as a scientist, can really appreciate. A bomb weighing only a few hundred pounds—and much of that is mechanism and not explosive U-235 or other materials—has equaled the total bomb load of many hundreds of our greatest bombers carrying conventional missiles.

Fortunately, there is a great promise of good for the future in this news we have just had. When this dreadful war is over, the same process can be turned to the improvement of the lot of mankind. But there must be supervision—there must be rigid and thorough supervision by every national and international agreement we can possibly arrive at. And, with such supervision and proper use, I can foresee within my lifetime that we shall no longer have to grub so furiously in the Earth to bring up coal and oil. We can use atomic power to turn the turbine in our power plants. In medicine, too, there will be many applications of the cyclotron and its work. Radiation from artificially radioactive atoms, assembled in the laboratory, can be used in treating the ills of mankind. It's a dreadful thing today, but in it there is great hope and great promise for the future.

Operation Crossroads

In July 1946, the government conducted a series of atomic tests in the Bikini Atoll, part of the Micronesian Islands in the Pacific Ocean. Known as Operation Crossroads, the tests consisted of two atomic detonations: Able (Test "A" air burst) and Baker (Test "B" underwater burst). On hand were some 90 ships, more than 40,000 observers, and assorted test animals. The intent, even though the Soviet Union was three years away from exploding its own atomic bomb, was to study the impact of the bomb on the U.S. military and naval forces and to develop procedures for protecting ships and personnel. The Joint Chiefs of Staff Evaluation Board issued its second preliminary report to the public on July 30, 1946.

Section I:
Supplement to Preliminary Report on Test "A"

In general, the observations on ship damage presented by this board in its first report were confirmed by engineering surveys. The location of the bomb burst, accurately determined from photographs, was such that only one ship was within 1,000 feet of the surface point over which the bomb exploded. There were about 20 ships within half a mile, all of which were badly damaged, many being put out of action and five sunk. It required up to 12 days to repair all of those ships left afloat sufficiently so that they could have steamed under their own power to a major base for repair.

It is now possible to make some estimate of the radiological injuries which crews would have suffered had they been aboard Test "A" target vessels. Measurements of radiation intensity and a study of animals exposed in ships show that the initial flash of principal lethal radiations, which are gamma-rays and neutrons, would have killed almost all personnel normally stationed aboard the ships centered around the air burst and many others at greater distances. Personnel protected by steel, water, or other dense materials would have been relatively safe in the outlying target vessels. The effects of radiation exposure would not have incapacitated all victims immediately, even some of the most severely affected might have remained at their stations several hours. Thus, it is possible that initial efforts at damage control might have kept ships operating, but it is clear that vessels within a mile of an atomic bomb air burst would eventually become inoperative due to crew casualties.

Operation Crossroads, conducted in the Bikini Islands in July 1946, involved more than 40,000 observers, some 90 ships, and numerous test animals. Test A, an air burst, proved that most people close to the explosion would have been killed instantly from the blast, heat, and lethal radiation; however, personnel protected by steel or other dense materials on outlying vessels away from the blast would have been relatively safe, according to the government's report (National Archives).

Section II:
Observation on Test "B"

The Board divided into two groups for the observation of Test "B." Four members, after surveying the target array from the air, witnessed the explosion from an airplane eight miles away at an altitude of 7,500 feet. The other three members inspected the target array from a small boat the day before the test and observed the bomb's explosion from the dock of the USS *Haven*, 11 miles at sea to the east of the burst.

The Board reassembled on the *Haven* on 26 July, and the members have since examined photographs, data on radioactivity, and reports of other phenomena, and have inspected some of the target vessels. They have also consulted with members of the Task Force Technical Staff.

As scheduled, at 0835 Bikini time on 25 July, a bomb was detonated well below the surface of the lagoon. This bomb was suspended from LSM-60, near the center of the

Test B was an underwater atomic explosion with a destructive power of 20,000 tons of TNT. This explosion sprayed highly lethal radioactive water onto ships located nearby. In contrast to the air burst explosion, Test B turned the contaminated ships into "radioactive stoves" and "would have burned all living things about them with invisible and painless but deadly radiation" (National Archives).

target array. The explosion was of predicted violence and is estimated to have been at least as destructive as 20,000 tons of TNT.

To a degree which the Board finds remarkable, the visible phenomena of explosion followed the predictions made by civilian and several phenomenologists attached to Joint Task Force One. At the moment of explosion, a dome, which showed the light of incandescent material within, rose upon the surface of the lagoon. The blast was followed by an opaque cloud which rapidly enveloped about half of the target array. The cloud vanished in about two seconds to reveal, as predicted, a column of ascending water. From some of the photographs, it appears that this column lifted the 26,000-ton battleship *Arkansas* for a brief interval before the vessel plunged to the bottom of the lagoon. Confirmation of this occurrence must await the analysis of high-speed photographs which are not yet available.

The diameter of the column of water was about 2,200 feet, and it rose to a height of about 5,500 feet. Spray rose to a much greater height. The column contained roughly ten million tons of water. For several minutes after the column reached maximum height, water fell back, forming an expanding cloud of spray which engulfed about half of the target array. Surrounding the base of the column was a wall of foaming water several hundred feet high.

Waves outside the water column, about 1,000 feet from the center of explosion, were 80 to 100 feet in height. These waves rapidly diminished in size as they proceeded outward, the highest wave reaching the beach of Bikini Island being seven feet. Waves did not pass over the island, and no material damage occurred there. Measurements of the underwater shock wave are not yet available. There were no seismic phenomena of significant magnitude.

The explosion produced intense radioactivity in the waters of the lagoon. Radioactivity immediately after the burst is estimated to have been the equivalent of many hundred tons of radium. A few minutes' exposure to this intense radiation at its peak would, within a brief interval, have incapacitated human beings and have resulted in their death within days or weeks.

Great quantities of radioactive water descended upon the ships from the column or were thrown over them by waves. This highly lethal radioactive water constituted such a hazard that after four days it was still unsafe for inspection parties, operating within a well-established safety margin, to spend any useful length of time at the center of the target area or to board ships anchored there.

As in Test "A," the array of target ships for Test "B" did not represent a normal anchorage but was designed instead to obtain the maximum data from a single explosion. Of the 84 ships and small craft in the array, 40 were anchored within one mile and 20 within about one-half mile. Two major ships were sunk, the battleship *Arkansas* immediately and the heavy-hulled aircraft carrier *Saratoga* after 7½ hours. A landing ship, a landing craft, and an oiler also sank immediately. The destroyer *Hughes*, in sinking condition, and the transport *Falcon*, badly listing, were later beached. The submerged submarine *Apogon* was sent to the bottom omitting air bubbles and fuel oil, and one to three other submerged submarines are believed to have sunk. Five days after the burst, the badly damaged Japanese battleship *Nagato* sank. It was found impossible immediately to assess damage to hulls, power plants, and machinery of the target ships because of radioactive contamination. Full appraisal of damage will have to await detailed survey by engineer teams. External observation from a safe distance would indicate that a few additional ships near the target center may have suffered some hull damage. There was no obvious damage to ships more than one-half miles from the burst.

Section III:
Observations and Conclusions, Both Tests

The operations of Joint Task Force One in conducting the tests have set a pattern for close, effective cooperation of the Armed Services and civilian scientists in the planning and execution of this highly technical operation. Moreover, the tests have provided valuable training of personnel in joint operations requiring great precision and coordination of effort.

It is impossible to evaluate an atomic burst in terms of conventional explosives. As to detonation and blast effects, where the largest bomb of the past was effective within a radius of a few hundred feet, the atomic bomb's effectiveness can be measured in thousands of feet. However, the radiological effects have no parallel in conventional weapons. It is necessary that a conventional bomb score a direct hit or a near miss of not more than a few feet to cause significant damage to a battleship. At Bikini, the second bomb, bursting under water, sank a battleship immediately at a distance of well over 500 feet. It damaged an aircraft carrier so that it sank in a few hours, while another battleship sank after five days. The first bomb, bursting in air, did great harm to the superstructures of major ships within a half-mile radius, but did only minor damage to their hulls. No ship within a mile of either burst could have escaped without some damage to itself and serious injury to a large number of its crew.

Although lethal results might have been more or less equivalent, the radiological phenomena accompanying the two bursts were markedly different. In the case of the air-burst bomb, it seems certain that unprotected personnel within one mile would have suffered high casualties by intense neutron and gamma radiation, as well as by blast and heat. Those surviving immediate effects would not have been menaced by radioactivity persisting after the blast.

In the case of the underwater explosion, the air-burst wave was far less intense and there was no heat wave of significance. Moreover, because of the absorption of neutrons and gamma rays by water, the lethal quality of the first flash of radiation was not of high order. But the second bomb threw large masses of highly radioactive water onto the decks and into the hulls of vessels. These contaminated ships became radioactive stoves, and would have burned all living things aboard them with invisible and painless but deadly radiation.

It is too soon to attempt an analysis of all of the implications of the Bikini tests. But it is not too soon to point to the necessity for immediate and intensive research into several unique problems posed by the atomic bomb. The poisoning of large volumes of water presents such a problem. Study must be given to procedures for protecting not only ships' crews but also the populations of cities against such radiological effects as were demonstrated in Bikini lagoon.

Observations during the two tests have established the general types and range of effectiveness of air and shallow underwater atomic-bomb bursts on naval vessels, army material, including a wide variety of Quartermaster stores, and personnel. From these observations and from instrumental data, it will now be possible to outline such changes, not only in military and naval design but also in strategy and tactics, as future events may indicate.

Understanding the Atomic Bomb

After the Soviet Union detonated its own atomic bomb in September 1949, the country's emphasis shifted from the awesome power of the atomic bomb to the very real possibility of an atomic war. In 1950, the New York State Civil Defense Commission issued You and the Atomic Bomb: What to Do in Case of an Atomic Attack, Public Pamphlet No. 1, *which helped set the tone for the next phase of the Atomic Age.*

We hope that your closest acquaintance with an atomic bomb will be in reading this pamphlet. But if you are to understand what to do if an A-bomb should fall on your city, you must first know what an A-bomb does.

An atomic bomb set off in mid-air, about 2,000 feet from ground level, is more destructive than either a water or ground burst, so we must consider this kind of attack as the most likely.

Air Burst

Here is what happens in an air burst: at the instant of the explosion, a brilliant fireball appears in the sky and quickly grows to about 900 feet in diameter. It could probably be seen for 50 miles in daylight, 200 miles at night. From this fireball, brighter than 100 suns, deadly heat and radiation burst out in all directions. The heat flash is dangerous up to 2 miles, but the radiation intensity falls off rapidly after 4,000 feet. In the first second, half of the radiation has already passed. In three seconds, heat and most of harmful radiation are over.

Following the heat flash, a tremendous shock wave caused by the expansion of hot gases from the explosion sweeps over the area. Winds of 800 mph accompany the shock wave in its early stages but fall off rapidly in intensity, dropping to 100 mph within a mile and a half. Several seconds later, another wind roars in toward the center of the explosion with about half the force of the out-rushing blast. At the end of 10 seconds, the immediate danger from the explosion itself has passed.

If you are above ground anywhere within three quarters of a mile from the air burst, you will have less than a 50-50 chance of survival. If you are underground within this area, you will have a good chance of coming through, unless you are almost directly under the point where the bomb explodes.

Here are some estimates of how an atomic explosion would damage the area around it:

Within one-half mile—Complete devastation. Little chance of survival if above ground.

From one-half to one mile—All buildings, except those of concrete and heavy steel frame, will be gutted or destroyed. The heat flash will be intense, but radiation will be reduced.

From one mile to a mile and a half—Most old-style brick and frame buildings will be destroyed. Modern buildings will be seriously damaged. There will be great danger from flying debris. Radiation will no longer be a hazard. The heat flash will still be dangerous, but not lethal.

Hundreds of scattered fires will break out, many of them caused by broken gas mains, oil lines and tanks or shorted electric circuits. All utilities will be destroyed or seriously damaged.

At two miles—Damage here will almost all be due to blast and secondary fires. Public utilities will be badly damaged. Only moderate burns, if any, will be caused by the heat flash.

At four miles—There will still be some blast damage, especially to frame and old-style wooden buildings, and scattered secondary fires. Rubble will block the streets.

Beyond four miles—In some instances, blast damage might extend to a distance of 6 miles, depending upon the wind, weather, and the terrain. Glass and plaster breakage might occur up to a distance of 8 miles. Utilities might be disrupted from damage in the central blast area.

About a half hour after the explosion, a strong wind will blow in toward the center of the damaged area, spreading the fires that have already been started.

You and the Atomic Bomb, Public Pamphlet #1, New York State Civil Defense Commission, 1950.

As Operations Crossroads verified, ground and water bursts were especially lethal because they created radioactive clouds of dust and spray, and these clouds were then carried by winds to affect people far from the initial blast.

Ground and Water Bursts

While it is likely that an enemy will prefer an air burst because of the greater damage it does, he may deliberately or accidentally explode an atomic bomb on the ground or in a harbor.

In ground or water burst, the effects of the blast, heat, and direct radiation do not extend nearly as far as in an air burst. In the case of a water burst, heat and direct radiation are negligible, and heavy damage from the shock wave does not extend beyond one mile.

However, both ground and water bursts have a particular danger of their own which is almost completely lacking in air bursts. The clouds of spray or dust thrown into the air by these bursts become highly radioactive. As they drift with the wind over the surrounding area, they contaminate all objects in their path and poison people who are exposed to them too long.

Radiation

You need not worry about lingering radioactivity after an air burst. It is now known that there is much less residual radiation from an atomic air burst than was at first feared.

Americans understood the drill: When you see a blinding flash, cover yourself ... quickly. Wearing a hat helped protect you from initial radiation, but not enough if you were too close to the blast.

But a ground or water burst leaves a great amount of deadly radioactivity behind in the spray or dirt that spreads contamination as it falls to earth. Radiation, even if you have absorbed a considerable amount of it, is not always fatal, however.

There is no immediate way of knowing when you have been exposed to radiation during or after the atomic burst. You will not feel anything if radiation hits you. Signs of radiation sickness show up later. How much later depends upon how much radiation you have absorbed.

If you have absorbed a large amount, you will know it within a few hours. The first signs are nausea and shock.

In the first day or two, the shock will be followed by vomiting, diarrhea, and fever. There will be no pain, but you will suffer discomfort, depression, and fatigue.

The symptoms will disappear, then return for two or three days. In the *worst* and *untreated* cases, death follows.

In moderate cases, these symptoms will appear only after several days — in some cases two or three weeks. During this time the mouth and gums will bleed, and there will be internal bleeding. All bleeding, even from small cuts, will be difficult to stop. Loss of appetite and falling hair also may indicate radiation sickness.

Medical Attention Important

In many cases, radiation sickness symptoms disappear entirely for a time. This does not mean you are out of danger. The symptoms may return at a later time.

If you show any signs of radiation sickness or have reason to believe the area you have been in is radioactive, go to a medical station at once.

Conditions after the bombing, however, may not permit you to get proper medical treatment immediately. In this case, follow these simple rules until help comes: Keep warm. Get complete rest; stay in bed if possible. Drink warm, nourishing liquids and eat foods rich in sugar and protein, but do not eat or drink foods or liquids that have been exposed in a contaminated area.

SIX SURVIVAL SECRETS FOR ATOMIC ATTACKS

ALWAYS PUT FIRST THINGS FIRST AND

1. TRY TO GET SHIELDED

If you have time, get down in a basement or subway. Should you unexpectedly be caught out-of-doors, seek shelter alongside a building, or jump in any handy ditch or gutter.

2. DROP FLAT ON GROUND OR FLOOR

To keep from being tossed about and to lessen the chances of being struck by falling and flying objects, flatten out at the base of a wall, or at the bottom of a bank.

3. BURY YOUR FACE IN YOUR ARMS

When you drop flat, hide your eyes in the crook of your elbow: That will protect your face from flash burns, prevent temporary blindness and keep flying objects out of your eyes.

NEVER LOSE YOUR HEAD AND

4. DON'T RUSH OUTSIDE RIGHT AFTER A BOMBING

After an air burst, wait a few minutes then go help to fight fires. After other kinds of bursts wait at least 1 hour to give lingering radiation some chance to die down.

5. DON'T TAKE CHANCES WITH FOOD OR WATER IN OPEN CONTAINERS

To prevent radioactive poisoning or disease, select your food and water with care. When there is reason to believe they may be contaminated, stick to canned and bottled things if possible.

6. DON'T START RUMORS

In the confusion that follows a bombing, a single rumor might touch off a panic that could cost your life.

Remove this sheet and keep it with you until you've memorized it.

Survival Under Atomic Attack, National Security Resources Board, Civil Defense Office, 1950.

Part 2

Radioactive Fallout

Your Civil Defense Manual: A Handbook on Personal Survival, Milwaukee Civil Defense Administration, American Radio Publications, no date.

From "Initial" to "Lingering" Fallout

If you were unfortunate enough to be close to ground zero, "initial" or explosive fallout would be fatal; "lingering" fallout, on the other hand, might affect you weeks or even months later. Survival Under Atomic Attack, *published by the National Security Resources Board, Civil Defense Office, in 1950, explained the radiation dangers resulting from an atomic explosion — a year after the Soviet Union entered the Atomic Age.*

In all stories about atomic weapons, there is a great deal about radioactivity.

Radioactivity is the only way — besides size — in which the effects of A or H bombs are different from ordinary bombs. But, with the exception of underwater or ground explosions, the radioactivity from atomic bursts is much less to be feared than blast and heat.

Radioactivity is not new or mysterious. In the form of cosmic rays from the sky, all of us have been continually bombarded by radiation every hour and day of our lives. We all have also breathed and eaten very small amounts of radioactive materials without even knowing it. For over half a century, doctors and scientists have experimented and worked with X-rays and other penetrating forms of energy. Because of all this experience, we actually know much more about radioactivity and what it does to people than we know about infantile paralysis, colds, or some other common diseases.

It is easy to understand how radioactivity works if we think of how sunlight behaves.

In the northern part of the world, winter's slanting sun rays seldom cause sunburn, but the hotter rays of the summer sun often do. Still, just a few moments in the midsummer sun will not give you a tan or sunburn. You have to stay in its hot rays for some time before you get a burn. What's more, bad sunburn on just the face and hands may hurt, but it won't seriously harm you. On the other hand, if it covers your whole body, it can make you very sick, or sometimes even cause death.

In the same way, the harm that can come to you from radioactivity will depend on the power of the rays and particles that strike you, upon the length of time you are exposed to them, and on how much of your body is exposed.

What Is "Initial" Radioactivity?

Broadly speaking, atomic explosions produce two different kinds of radioactivity. First — and most important in an air burst — is an extremely powerful invisible burst of

Survival Under Atomic Attack, National Security Resources Board, Civil Defense Office, 1950.

rays and particles thrown off at the time of explosion. This kind is called "initial" or explosive radioactivity. Its rays and particles fly out quickly, then promptly die. There is danger from them only for little more than a minute. The second type of radioactivity — lingering radioactivity — will be described later.

The injury range of the explosive radioactivity from a modern A-bomb is a little over 1 mile, if the bomb is exploded about 2,000 feet in the air. If it is exploded much higher, some of the radioactivity may not reach the ground, so the range may be less. If it is exploded much lower, the radiation also may not reach out as far, because it would be blocked by the ground or by buildings.

A little more than a mile away, the principal effects of the few dying rays that struck you could be seen only as temporary blood changes in a doctor's examination. You probably wouldn't even realize you had been exposed.

A little less than a mile from the explosion center, if you are unprotected, you are almost sure to suffer illness. Less than two-thirds of a mile away, those caught in the open are pretty sure to soak up a fatal dose of radioactivity.

Still, the possibility of your being caught without some protection is not very great. Even if you are on the street, there is a good chance that a building, or many buildings, will be between you and the burst, and they will partially or completely shield you.

Atomic explosions high above ground cause the most widespread damage. And, as happened in Japan, when an A-bomb goes off in the air you are far more likely to be hurt by the bomb's blast and heat waves than by its radioactivity. At Hiroshima and Nagasaki, slightly over one-half of all deaths and injuries were caused by blast. Nearly one-third of the casualties were from the heat flash. *Radioactivity alone caused only about 15 percent of all deaths and injuries.*

If the bomb were to go off close to the ground, or slightly below its surface, the range of the explosive radiation, as well as the range of the blast and heat, would be reduced. This is due to the fact that all three would be partially blocked by the earth, by nearby buildings, and by other obstacles.

In an underwater burst, there would be much less to fear from blast and nothing to fear from heat. Practically all the explosive radioactivity would be absorbed by the water. However, there would be the second type of radioactivity to be described later on.

What About "Induced" Radioactivity?

If an atomic bomb goes off in the air within two-thirds of a mile or slightly more of your home, there is no practical way of keeping explosive radioactivity out of the above-ground part of your house. It is possible that, at very short range, artificial, or induced, radioactivity could be set up in gold, silver, and many other objects. However, this kind of radioactivity will never offer great danger, so don't throw away bandages and other first aid materials in the medicine cabinet. They will be perfectly safe to use.

Naturally, the radioactivity that passes through the walls of your house won't be stopped by tin or glass. It can go right through canned and bottled foods. However, this will not make them dangerous, and it will not cause them to spoil. Go ahead and use them, provided the containers are not broken open.

What About "Radiation Sickness"?

Should you be caught upstairs or in the open at the time of a bombing, you might soak up a serious dose of explosive radioactivity. Even so, the first indication that you had been pierced by the rays probably wouldn't show up for a couple of hours. Then you most likely would get sick at your stomach and begin to vomit. However, you might be sick at your stomach for other reasons, too, so vomiting won't always mean you have radiation sickness. The time it would take you to get sick would depend on how strong a dose you got. The stronger the dose, the quicker you would get sick. For a few days you might continue to feel below par and about 2 weeks later most of your hair might fall out. By the time you lost your hair, you would be good and sick. But in spite of it all, you would still stand better than an even chance of making a complete recovery, including having your hair grow in again.

What About Lingering Radioactivity?

Knowing how to protect yourself from blast, heat, and explosive radioactivity, only one major problem remains: That is how to avoid harm from lingering radioactivity.

Explosive radioactivity bursts from the bomb at the time of explosion and lasts only little more than a minute.

Lingering radioactivity remains for a longer time, from a few minutes to weeks or months, depending on the kind of radioactive material.

Lingering radioactivity may become a danger when atomic bombs are exploded on the ground, underground, or in the water. Air bursts leave no dangerous lingering radioactivity.

Most lingering radioactivity comes from leftover bomb wastes, or "ashes," technically called fission products. They consist of countless billions of fragments, or pieces, of atoms split up in the explosion. Smaller, and usually less dangerous, amounts of lingering radioactivity may be thrown off by scattered atoms of uranium or plutonium that fail to split up when the bomb goes off.

These totally invisible radioactivity particles act much the same as ordinary, everyday dust. When present in any real quantity, they are scattered about in patches and contaminate, or pollute, everything they fall on, including people. While they can be removed easily from some surfaces, they stick very tightly to others. It is practically impossible to get absolutely all of them out of household corners and cracks. Most of the time, it is far easier to prevent pollution than it is to remove it.

What About Protecting Yourself from Lingering Radioactivity?

While attempting to avoid exposure to the bomb's blast, heat, and explosive radioactivity, also do what you can to keep from being showered by radioactive waste materials. Inside a shelter or building, there is little or nothing to fear from this source. But if caught out-of-doors, try to grab hold of something to cover yourself with when you fall to the ground. A board or some sheets of newspaper might help, but a raincoat would be better. The object is, of course, to keep radioactive dust and raindrops off your body and clothing. When it's safe to get up, throw away your covering.

Always do what you can to help other people. There is no chance of your being harmed by radioactivity from the bodies of others, even if they have radiation injuries. Don't leave injured people where they may be burned. Direct rescue workers to persons trapped in the wreckage. If necessary to bandage open cuts and wounds and no standard first aid equipment is available, use parts of your own or the victim's clothing. But tear them from the under, not the outer garments. Underclothes are far less likely to be contaminated by radioactivity.

If you have walked through rubble from a ground burst or water from an underwater burst, be sure to change at least your outer garments and shoes. Outer clothes will automatically serve as a "trap" for most of the radioactivity you may accidentally pick up. By taking them off, you will remove most of the contamination. If the clothing is heavily contaminated, it is best to bury it.

You also should manage to take a bath or shower, if you have been in an area of lingering radioactivity. It is important that all radioactive materials be removed as soon as possible from your body, and bathing is the only practical means of getting rid of them. You won't need special cleaning compounds. Warm water and soap are ideal.

In washing, pay particular attention to your hair, for that is one place where the wastes are sure to pile up. Also give your hands a good scrubbing and get all dirt out from under your fingernails. If there is a radiological defense man handy, have him check you with his meter after you've finished your clean-up. Should he find your body still radioactive, again scrub yourself from head to foot. Then do it a third time if necessary. You can remove practically all of the radioactivity if you keep at it.

Remember all this is necessary only for persons who have come in contact with radioactive materials in heavily contaminated areas.

FACTS about fallout

IT COULD HIT YOU!

WHOM WILL IT HIT?

Fallout is nothing more than particles of matter in the air, made radioactive by nuclear or thermonuclear explosions. When an atomic or hydrogen bomb is exploded close to the ground, thousands of tons of atomized earth, building materials, rocks, and gases are sucked upward, sometimes to a height of 80,000 feet or more. They help form the mushroom cloud which is always seen with one of these explosions.

Some of these radioactive particles spill out in the immediate area of the explosion soon after it occurs, but others may be carried by the upper winds for many miles. Sooner or later, however, they settle to earth. This is called fallout.

WHO, ME?

HOW WILL I KNOW IT?

HERE'S HOW YOU'LL KNOW IT

YOU CAN'T SMELL IT
YOU CAN'T TASTE IT
YOU CAN'T HEAR IT
YOU CAN'T TOUCH IT

Civil Defense officials and weather experts will estimate the probable path and speed of approaching fallout. Tune your AM Radio to 640 or 1240 kc, your Conelrad stations for official C. D. news and instructions. Fallout can settle anywhere. Small towns and rural areas many miles from the scene of a nuclear explosion are potential fallout targets, and as such must organize for self-protection, as well as to learn how to care for evacuees. If you live in a rural area, prepare NOW by surveying your home and outbuildings to determine how many you can accommodate. Consult your local Civil Defense for instructions on mass feeding techniques.

Source: Facts About Fallout — FCDA

***Your Civil Defense Manual: A Handbook on Personal Survival**, Milwaukee Civil Defense Administration, no date.*

Nuclear Fallout

By the mid–1950s, with both the United States and the Soviet Union flexing their nuclear capabilities, no American was completely immune from radioactive fallout, which could now affect people hundreds of miles from ground zero. Understanding the expanded dangers of fallout, including residual fallout, was covered in What You Should Know About Radioactive Fallout, *published by the Federal Civil Defense Administration in 1958.*

Since early 1954, most of us have heard or read stories about a product of nuclear explosions called "radioactive fallout."

Many people who passed on those stories knew only that fallout had something to do with our atomic tests in the Pacific, and that Japanese fishermen many miles from the test site were made ill by it.

In some minds, fallout began to take on all the terrors of the unknown. This was not surprising, because people are always inclined to fear what they do not fully understand.

At first it was hard for many people to understand this new danger in its true perspective, because there were only rumors and conflicting reports. In February 1955, President Eisenhower decided that the story of fallout could be told to the American people without revealing valuable information to a possible enemy. The President approved public announcement of the facts about fallout by the Atomic Energy Commission and the Federal Civil Defense Administration.

It is true that radioactive fallout is a new peril to civilian populations in this air-atomic age. Radiation itself is nothing new or mysterious. We encounter some radiation every day in one form or another.

Since the beginning of time, all living things have been exposed to radioactivity from natural sources. Cosmic rays from the sky bombard us with small amounts of radiation every minute of our lives. All of us have breathed and eaten mildly radioactive materials without knowing it or feeling any effects.

Our surroundings have always contained some radioactive elements. We receive radiation exposure when we have X-rays taken. Our luminous watch dials are radioactive. From long experience, our doctors and scientists know a great deal about radiation. Because they understand its limits and effects, we can defend ourselves against radioactive fallout.

The purpose of this book is to tell you what you should know about fallout. You will learn what causes fallout when a nuclear weapon is detonated, when and where it may be expected to occur, and protective measures you can take.

What you should know about RADIOACTIVE FALLOUT

FEDERAL CIVIL DEFENSE ADMINISTRATION

PA-B-7 (Revised May 1958).

What You Should Know About Radioactive Fallout, Federal Civil Defense Administration, revised May 1958.

What Is Fallout?

The term "fallout" is used to describe radioactive material produced by a nuclear explosion.

This material is composed of particles of dirt, stone, and other debris carried into the upper air by the force of the explosion. The particles are contaminated by radioactive products of the bomb, and fall back to earth over a wide area.

Many of the radioactive particles are carried up as much as 80,000 feet in the familiar mushroom-shaped cloud. From this cloud the particles spread downwind over hundreds of square miles. In the first few hours, the prevailing winds carry the fallout particles along while they lose some of their radioactivity. Eventually, they return to the earth, but they can still be dangerous to you. Some of these particles are heavy enough to fall to the ground while they are still intensely radioactive.

How Can You Detect Fallout?

Radioactive fallout *could* be visible in your area in the form of dust. On a clear day, the direction in which the mushroom cloud was moving *might* give you some warning of its approach. Radioactivity is not something that you can detect by smell, touch, or taste. Each particle is like a small X-ray machine. The only way to detect a dangerous fallout area is by radiological monitoring. Officials will warn you by radio and other means if your area is not safe, and then you can take the protective measures described in this booklet.

Where Would Fallout Occur?

Authorities can predict the probable areas of fallout after a nuclear attack, but they cannot accurately say how serious it will be. The size of the bomb, height at which it is exploded, nature of the ground below, and weather and wind conditions will determine these things.

The U.S. Weather Bureau issues fallout forecasts at least twice a day (four times a day in some areas). The forecasts cover all critical target areas of the country. The predictions can be useful for emergency planning and alerting people to take shelter. Because of the limitations of the system, the forecast should not be the basis for ordering evacuation.

The thing to do is to follow official instructions after an attack has occurred. You can rely on official information. If a nuclear weapon explodes in your area, tune to 640 and 1240 on your AM radio dial.

Characteristics of Nuclear Explosions

The effects of any nuclear explosion are (1) blast, (2) heat, (3) initial radiation, and (4) *residual* radiation. The first three occur together, at the time of the explosion.

Residual radiation from fallout is different. It falls back to earth over a much larger area than is affected by blast, heat, or initial radiation, and can continue to be dangerous over a considerable period of time. Its presence is not always immediately evident to its victims, and its intensity will vary from one place to another within the same fallout pattern.

An enemy would not be likely to explode a nuclear weapon as a high air burst. He would probably fire it as a surface burst. The greater quantity of radioactive fallout thus resulting would make this bomb much more effective over a larger area.

Fallout Area

It is impossible to know in advance how large or where the area of dangerous fallout would be. During the 1954 tests in the Pacific, the fallout that showered Japanese fishermen was radioactive enough to dangerously contaminate an area extending downwind for 220 miles and varying in width up to 40 miles. This cigar-shaped area would have been large enough to reach from Washington, D.C., to New York City, including the cities of Baltimore, Wilmington, Philadelphia, and Trenton.

Where Does Fallout Start?

The larger radioactive particles from a nuclear explosion start to fall out shortly after the bomb is fired. Coarse, heavy particles fall faster and settle closer to the point of the explosion.

An accurate timetable cannot be set up for fallout particles because they are affected by many things. Fallout may begin at once in your area, or it may not begin for some time afterward, depending upon your distance from the point where the bomb is dropped, the size of the bomb, wind conditions in the upper air, and the presence of snow, rain, or other atmospheric conditions.

How Long Is Fallout Dangerous?

Radiation from fallout does not remain a hazard indefinitely. Fallout radioactivity decreases with time, rapidly at first and then more slowly. The longer the cloud is in the air, and the farther it travels from the point of explosion, the less danger there is because radioactivity is reduced, and the particles are dispersed over a wider area. The greatest danger is during the first day or two. Two days after the explosion, the rate of radiation per hour of fallout is only about $\frac{1}{100}$th of the rate in the first hour after the burst. Even after that period, the danger continues. Radioactivity is a long-range problem. Lengthy exposure to low level radiation can still make you ill.

Who Is Endangered by Fallout?

Before the fallout effects of the 1954 nuclear explosion were announced, people living in the country, or in small urban communities far from our target cities, could consider themselves safe from the direct effects of enemy bombing. This is no longer true.

The first Pacific nuclear test showed us that deadly radioactive fallout can be carried a very great distance. Lethal radiation occurred nearly 200 miles from the center of that explosion.

Most of us in this country live within fallout range of some target which it might be important for the enemy to destroy. This means that every one of us could be exposed to fallout hazard if an enemy should attack. Every American should know what to do about this danger.

Defenses Against Fallout

There are only two defenses against radioactive fallout. One is not to be in an area where fallout occurs. The other is to be protected from fallout by adequate shelter.

Since no one can tell, until fallout has occurred and is monitored for radioactivity, where the dangerous areas will be, there is no way you can put the first defense to practical use. Evacuating your home, solely on the basis of a fallout prediction, might prove unwise since it might result in going to an area where the contamination was more dangerous and less shelter was available than at home.

Millions of persons may be evacuated from target cities if attack is expected, but the primary purpose of this evacuation will be to remove civilians from the areas of blast and fire damage.

After fallout occurs, there are two additional defenses against the dangerous effects of radioactivity.

The first is remedial evacuation from areas where monitoring shows that it is unsafe to remain, because radioactivity is so high that it will remain dangerous for a considerable period of time despite the decay factor. The second is to decontaminate the articles and the surroundings that threaten you with radiation exposure.

Decontamination

In discussing nuclear bombings, "decontamination" means getting rid of dangerous radioactivity.

The greatest danger from fallout radiation is from external exposure to radioactive material. Dust settling on your body or clothes is extremely hazardous. It is not likely that food and water inside a building would be contaminated and harmful to eat or drink. If there are quantities of dust in the air, precautions should be taken against breathing it.

There is no special clothing recommended for protection against fallout. Any clothing which keeps fallout from settling directly on your body provides some protection. The more of your body that is covered the better. Outer clothing can be removed after you reach shelter to rid yourself of most of the contamination you have picked up.

Washing will remove radioactive fallout from clothing and your person. However, the particles will still be in the water you use. Empty it away from places where people gather, and don't dump it near any source of drinking water.

If you cannot wash your exposed clothing immediately, bury or store it in a suitable place at a distance from your shelter.

Household Decontamination

Food or water in a closed refrigerator, covered containers, or sealed packages is safe to consume. The contents of packages left in the open will be all right if their covers are intact. Make sure that cans, bottles, or other containers have not been punctured or broken. Wash them off carefully before you open them. Boiling, which kills many kinds of contamination, has no effect whatsoever on radioactivity.

You may need to use your vacuum cleaner and its attachments to remove radioactive dust from the inside walls, furniture, and rugs. However, the contamination will then be concentrated in the dust receptacle. This will have to be removed and buried.

Outside Decontamination

You should wait until fallout has stopped and authorities have declared your area safe before you go outside. When you can work safely outside for an hour or two at a time, turn a hose on the roof and walls of your house. A heavy rainfall would have the same effect. Large areas of ground contaminated by fallout can be made safer by plowing or other operations that turn the surface under. These things should not be done until the authorities have instructed you to do them.

What the Government Does to Protect You from Fallout

The government is striving constantly to find the latest and best ways to protect you from radioactive fallout, as well as from other effects of a nuclear attack.

As planning and research develop new possibilities for protection, the government tests them. As new dangers arise, the government moves to meet them. Meanwhile, improved warning systems, operational exercises, and drills are steadily being pushed to enable you to take the best possible advantage of the defense methods that now exist.

RADIOACTIVITY IS NOTHING NEW...

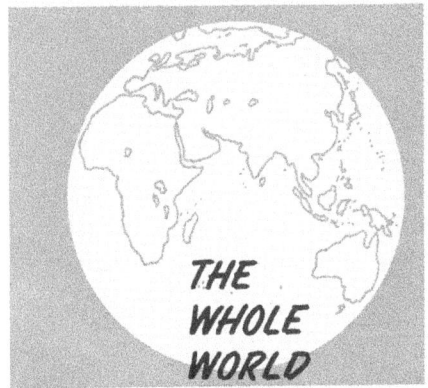

THE WHOLE WORLD IS RADIOACTIVE

But normal amounts are not dangerous. It is only when radioactivity is present in highly concentrated amounts, such as those created by atomic and hydrogen bomb explosions, that it becomes dangerous. Radioactive fallout is sometimes highly concentrated.

If you are exposed to it long enough—

IT WILL HURT YOU!

IT MAY EVEN KILL YOU!

WHOM WILL IT HIT?

IT COULD HIT YOU!

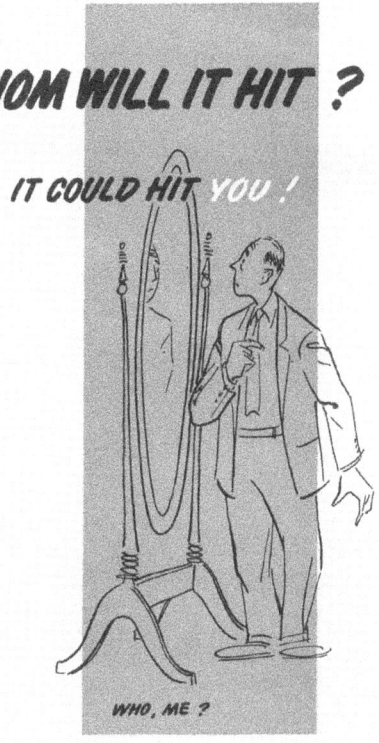

WHO, ME?

Yes, it could settle anywhere. The upper winds could carry fallout to the most remote parts of the country. Small towns and rural areas many miles from the scene of a nuclear explosion may be endangered by fallout. Every citizen is a potential target for fallout.

Facts About Fallout, Federal Civil Defense Administration, 1955.

Fallout on the Farm

Whether you lived in a city or on a farm, the need to understand the dangers of a nuclear bomb remained. In 1958, the U.S. Department of Agriculture issued Radioactive Fallout on the Farm *to answer a list of questions related to the effects of radioactivity on animals and food.*

Most Americans know about the destructive power of atomic and hydrogen bombs and other nuclear weapons. The explosive power of the atomic bombs used in World War II was equivalent to about 20,000 tons of TNT. Since then, bombs have been developed that have explosive power equivalent to millions of tons of TNT.

An enemy attack with a nuclear weapon could cause radioactive contamination many miles downwind from the target area. Radioactive particles produced by the bomb give off destructive rays, which, in certain situations, can injure — or kill — human beings and animals, and can make farm lands and crops dangerous to use. These particles are called radioactive fallout.

Fallout could settle anywhere — even in the most remote parts of the country. If large industrial centers were bombed with hydrogen weapons, it is likely that small towns and rural areas in the downwind path would be endangered.

Fallout may or may not be visible, and the radiation from the active elements can be detected only by special instruments. Because of this, you will be notified through regular government channels when your lands lie within the path of harmful radioactive contamination.

There is a defense against fallout — on the farm and in the home. The following questions and answers will help you to understand the nature of fallout, and, in the event of enemy attack, will help you protect yourself from it.

Fallout: Livestock

How will fallout affect unprotected livestock — that is, animals in fields, pastures, and other open areas?

Fallout may be dangerous to cattle, sheep, horses, pigs, and other livestock as well as to human beings. Animals can suffer skin burns if fallout settles in the coat. If animals drink fallout in their water or eat it in pasture grass or commercial feed, the radiation may cause serious internal injuries. Radioactive particles that contaminate the skin or the

FARMERS' BULLETIN No. 2107

DEFENSE AGAINST Radioactive Fallout on the farm

U. S. DEPARTMENT OF AGRICULTURE

Radioactive Fallout on the Farm, U.S. Department of Agriculture, 1958.

immediate environment emit rays capable of penetrating deep into the body and may result in total body exposure.

In you receive ample warming that fallout is coming, you can take certain precautions to protect your livestock and reduce losses. But once fallout occurs, you should not attempt to protect livestock unless authorities tell you that it is safe to do so.

What can I do with contaminated feed?

You may be able to feed it to livestock eventually. Because of radioactive decay, even dangerously contaminated feed may be safe to use after a period of storage. How long feed should be stored depends on such factors as the type of concentration of the fission products. Area monitors will notify farmers of these factors through regular Government channels.

Should dairy cows receive special treatment?

Yes. Since radioactive materials can accumulate in milk, which will be a very critical product during an emergency, you should make a special effort to protect cows from fallout.

Give cows preferred shelter and clean feed and water. If you can, milk them before fallout occurs. You may not be able to do so for a day or two afterwards. Reduce amounts of water and concentrated feed, and, if practicable, put cows and calves together; the calves can suckle and reduce the discomfort of full udders.

What animal food products are safe to market after fallout?

You will receive specific official instructions based on the amount of fallout received. *Do not destroy any animal food products unless spoilage has made them inedible.* Contaminated food products may be safe for consumption if they can be stored for a period of time to allow the radioactivity to decay.

What are the effects of fallout on growing vegetables?

Growing vegetables that are exposed to heavy fallout may become highly radioactive. Leaves, pods, and fruits are immediately contaminated upon contact with the radioactive particles. Roots and tubers are affected if they absorb long-lived materials, such as radioactive strontium, from the soil. Underground vegetables may become affected if they touch contaminated surface soil during harvest. Most vegetables would be marketable, and should not be destroyed without testing for radioactivity.

What special precautions should be taken for workers in the fields?

Everyone should remain indoors until the danger from fallout has diminished. When you are advised by local officials that it is safe to work outdoors, you may be asked to take certain precautions against collecting dust on your body, such as wearing boots, coat, hat, and gloves. If you work with livestock, touch them as little as possible; fallout may be on their backs.

More Pointers on Protection

If you have a few hours' warning...

Make arrangements for the safety of your family and yourself. Have about a 2 weeks' supply of food in the house.

Bring feed into buildings, or cover it with tarpaulin if it is left outdoors.

Store as much water as possible for livestock, especially if the water is coming from ponds or streams or through water mains. Cover wells and rain barrels.

Move farm machinery and equipment indoors or store them near the farm house and keep them covered.

If you have a few months' warning...

If the Government is able to give the public a few months' warning that an atomic attack is likely, here are some things you can do:

Put your silage pits and hay stacks near buildings and cover them with tarpaulins.

Keep your well clean and covered. Put some rainwater barrels and other containers near buildings; fill them regularly with clean water and keep them covered.

Store seed and grain in weatherproof buildings.

Stock up on packaged, canned, and bottled foods.

Have a satisfactory storage space for fuel.

Part 3

Women and the Home

Illustration used in numerous civil defense publications in the 1950s.

The Bomb and the Baby

An atomic bomb might annihilate your city, but, somehow, people could survive, including pregnant women. Assisting at the Birth of a Baby After Enemy Attack If No Doctor Is Available *provided the information needed when hospitals and doctors were not available. The New York State Department of Health published the booklet in 1954 on behalf of the New York State Civil Defense Commission.*

An atomic attack is known to cause the birth of many babies ahead of their expected time. This occurs because of the fear and exertion of the expectant mother. During the first 48 hours after an attack, medical or nursing care may not be available for deliveries (births) of babies — since all personnel will be working in medical installations caring for critically injured survivors. Hence, as many persons as possible should learn how to give care to the mother and baby.

Almost all births occur without trouble. But, there are many things a neighbor or member of the family can learn to do to help the mother and baby during delivery. In addition to learning how to care for normal deliveries, it is also necessary that persons learn how to recognize abnormal signs or symptoms which demand that the mother be seen by a doctor and hospitalized if necessary.

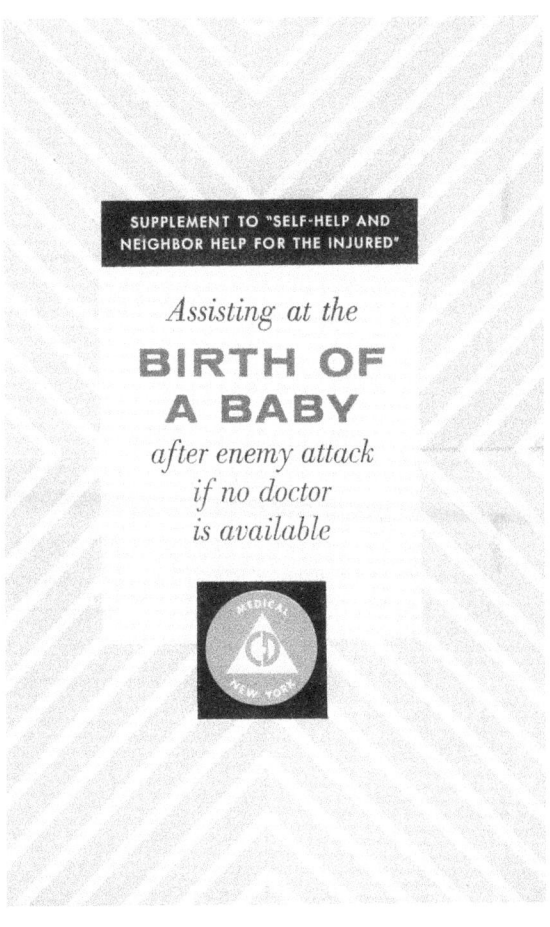

Assisting in the Birth of a Baby After Enemy Attack If No Doctor Is Available, New York State Department of Health, on behalf of the New York State Civil Defense Commission, 1954.

Broome County Office of Civil Defense

This is to Certify that

MARY DOOLITTLE

has satisfactorily completed the prescribed training
(POST ATTACK BIRTH OF A BABY)
and drill and is qualified to serve as a member of

the Medical *unit of Civil Defense*

DEPUTY DIRECTOR   DIRECTOR OF CIVIL DEFENSE

The New York State Civil Defense Commission offered training for the "Post Attack Birth of a Baby," complete with a certificate to signify the successful completion of the program and qualification to serve as a member of the Medical Unit of Civil Defense.

Care of the Baby

It is possible that in the confusion which will exist after an enemy attack, the mother and baby may be separated. For this reason some identifying information must be placed on the baby and mother. On a piece of smooth cloth write with a pen the father's and mother's full name, the date, sex of baby, time and place of the baby's birth, and tie it on the ankle or wrist of the baby. Tie it tight enough to stay on but not tight enough to stop circulation. Write the same information on another piece of cloth and tie it to the mother.

Do not wash the baby. The material which covers the baby at birth is a protection to the skin.

Women in Civil Defense

Women had a critical role in civil defense: to make sure the home was well equipped and the family was ready at any moment. Women in Civil Defense, *published in 1952 by the Federal Civil Defense Administration, outlined women's importance at home and in the community.*

Civil Defense Begins at Home

The home is the basic unit of the community — and the basic unit on which defense of the home front must be built.

Whether you are a housewife, secretary, business executive, or nurse, civil defense looks to you, as a woman, to take an active role in protecting your home. No one else can do that job for you.

Your first duty in civil defense is to act at once to educate your family in self-protection against modern weapons, and to make your home as safe as possible against the dangers of enemy attack.

Your second duty is to participate in your community civil defense organization. There must be a basic civil defense organization in each community in the United States, regardless of size or location. Without fully organized communities, there can be no adequate national civil defense program.

If your community does not have an active civil defense organization, much of the blame must fall on you and your neighbors. Unless you, as a responsible American woman, take action, you are gambling with the safety of your family, your friends, your community, and your country.

You would hardly blame others for failing to provide food, clothing, and shelter for your family. That is your family responsibility. And so is family civil defense. Community civil defense can be effective only if the families of the community are solidly behind it, willing to give time and effort to make it work. National civil defense can be only as effective as the people of the Nation make it.

Civil defense is here to stay. We will need it just as long as we need a strong military force. Without civil defense, no military force can win a major war.

This fact was recognized by Secretary of Defense Robert Lovett when he said that "civil defense is a co-equal partner" of the military forces.

In these days of atomic, biological, and chemical weapons carried by bombers, submarines, and agents, no part of America is beyond the reach of an enemy. What's more, we cannot prevent attack. General Vandenberg of the Air Force has said repeatedly that the *best* our anti-aircraft and interceptors will be able to do is to knock down 30 percent of attacking planes. Seven out of ten enemy planes will get through.

If this comes as a surprise, remember that our own air raids on Germany during the last war lost less, on the average, than one out of ten planes. *No enemy ever knocked down as much as 30 percent of our planes in any raid we ever made.* This was true even over Britain, Hamburg, or Schweinfurt.

Furthermore, an enemy would strike at our cities and our people first. This is true because our two greatest strengths are the civilian will to fight and to produce the sinews of war. To win a war, military forces must have a constant pipeline of supplies flowing to the fighting fronts. Civilians produce the things the military forces need. If our people, farms, and factories are destroyed, the military forces will soon have no supplies with which to fight.

And remember that American soldiers, sailors, airmen, and marines are fighting for the people at home. If the home front crumples behind them, they not only have nothing to fight *with*, they have nothing to fight *for*.

That's why civil defense is just as important as a strong military force and why civil defense is important to every community and person in America.

Not every community will be attacked. But those that are attacked cannot hope to take care of themselves without help. The help must come from the organized civil defense forces of communities and States which are not attacked. That's why *all* communities must be organized.

To do the job, over 17 million hard-working, well-trained volunteers are needed. Your community needs volunteers now and for years to come.

The greater percentage of these volunteers will be women like you.

At least 60 percent of civil defense volunteers must be women serving in hundreds of specialized civil defense jobs. Many volunteer jobs can be filled by you and your friends right now, with only a little training.

Women in Civil Defense, Federal Civil Defense Administration, 1952.

When you have trained your family and prepared your home, you have more than doubled your chances for survival in an atomic attack.

When you have joined in organizing your community, you have given the community and the Nation a far better chance to survive an enemy attack.

But you will have done more than just prepare in case of war — you will have made a positive contribution to keeping the peace.

An unprepared nation invites attack. A nation without civil defense is unprepared.

A strong civil defense preparedness program, like a strong military preparedness program, is not just a shield but a sword. Adequate civil defense preparedness can actually help hold the enemy at bay. If the enemy knows that he can demoralize us by an all-out attack on the home-front; if he knows that we are not prepared for it; if he knows that our civil defense system is ill-manned, ill-trained, and ill-equipped — this is a direct invitation to launch such an attack on our people and on our cities.

But, if Russia knows that millions of American men and women are well trained and organized and ready to move into action when the attack comes; if Russia knows that we have thousands of trained rescue squads and tens of thousands of wardens and millions of American families trained in first aid and self-protection; if Russia knows that we have this kind of adequate civil defense preparedness which would save at least half the American lives that might otherwise be lost — then Russia, or any other enemy, will think long and hard before launching an attack on this country.

The stronger we are in America in civil defense, the more Russian atomic bombs it will take to do the damage to our cities and people that the enemy must inflict in order to win a war.

Thus, a strong national civil defense program actually cuts down sharply the effectiveness of the enemy's stockpile of atomic bombs and his stockpile of other modern weapons.

Said quite simply, a strong American civil defense program forces Russia to use two atomic bombs instead of one, thus reducing the size and effectiveness of the Russian stockpile.

A strong civil defense stands side by side with our armed forces as a major deterrent to enemy attack on our own country. This makes civil defense a major force in helping keep the peace and in preventing World War III.

There is another value in civil defense which is becoming more apparent by the day — its peacetime use in natural disasters.

There have been many recent instances where the organization and training for civil defense in wartime have paid great dividends in meeting peacetime disasters; most all of the training you get in civil defense is useful in saving lives in peacetime, too.

Getting America prepared on the home front is a responsibility that falls in large part on the shoulders of all American women. It's your job — and you have no time to waste.

Family Civil Defense

Here are the simple steps you should take now to prepare your home and family against enemy attack:

1. Learn the civil defense air-raid alert signals.
2. Equip the most protected place you can find in or near your home for an air-raid shelter.
3. Learn the effects of an atomic explosion and the safety precautions you can take at home or at work to minimize danger and injury.
4. Prepare an emergency first-aid kit for your home.
5. Take a regular Red Cross first-aid or home nursing course as soon as you can.
6. Practice fire-proof housekeeping. Learn to fight fires in the home.
7. Get official civil defense identification tags for yourself and family, if available.
8. Learn the simple safety measures you and your family must take to protect yourself against germ and gas warfare.
9. Maintain a three-day supply of food and adequate water for use in an emergency.

Identification Tags

You should get identification tags for each member of your family from the local civil defense authorities.

Home Drills

Once you and the family have a basic knowledge of self-protection, you should hold air-raid drills and practice fire-fighting techniques. Give each member of the family a task in keeping with age and physical capabilities. Alternate duties as much as possible so that all members of the family are familiar with each air-raid and fire-fighting task. Hold drills frequently so that responses to emergency situations become automatic.

How Women's Organizations Can Help

Mobilization of the resources of this country's organized groups is essential to achieve the objective of 17 million volunteer workers. The majority of women's organizations have national, State, or local publications and programs. These are excellent for developing civil defense activities. Through these news organs, millions of American women can learn something about self-protection for themselves and their families and about civil defense generally.

Women's organizations also can contribute to the recruitment of civil defense volunteers by asking their members to register as ready and willing to participate. The jobs open to women in civil defense cover every phase of the operation, ranging from child-care aides in emergency welfare services to laboratory technicians in the health services. Before women will volunteer for these jobs, however, they must appreciate the need for civil defense and understand how it works. Here's how your organization can help.

Things to Do

Since civil defense depends on the active support of every man, woman, and child in this country, women's organizations should familiarize their members will the various aspects of civil defense. The organization members, once they have become informed, can use their knowledge to interest friends and neighbors who may not be club members. This knowledge will also help them to know which civil defense service they might qualify for with training.

If you are a member of a women's organization, work for the appointment of a civil defense chairman in your association. Once this office has been established, a committee should be formed to work with the chairman. Through the committee, the following action can be taken to implement the organization's civil defense program:

1. Adopt a resolution pledging the organization's active cooperation with the local civil defense office.
2. Contact local civil defense authorities and offer the organization's support and cooperation.
3. Register all members as potential civil defense volunteers, in cooperation with local civil defense officials.
4. Promote civil defense activities through forums, speeches, the press, radio, television, motion pictures, direct mail, exhibits, and individual contacts. These activities should be coordinated with the operations of the local civil defense office.
5. Schedule at least five minutes at every organization meeting in which to spotlight official civil defense activities.
6. Report progress regularly to the organization's members.
7. Set up a training program in cooperation with the local civil defense office.
8. Publicize all club civil defense activities.
9. Launch your civil defense participation program at a public gathering attended by representatives of the local civil defense office.

If your club or chapter is part of a regional or national organization, contact headquarters. You probably will find — if you are not already aware of it — that the national organization already has a civil defense program and can supply material and guidance.

We pray that another war will be averted and that the free world may have continuing peace. But we must back our prayers with our own efforts.

The strength and courage of American women is one of the Nation's greatest resources. If the women of this country will prepare with courage and determination, we will have the civil defense we need to be strong — and each woman who gives her time and effort to civil defense will be doing her part to keep the forces of communism in check, to prepare us against attack, and to help keep the peace.

AT HOME!!

are YOU prepared

CALL YOUR CIVIL DEFENSE
HEADQUARTERS FOR TRAINING

GOOD, CLEAN HOUSEKEEPING
IS CIVIL DEFENSE
HOUSEKEEPING

BE PREPARED

LEARN HOW
TO PREVENT
& FIGHT FIRES **NOW**

It Could Happen Here! Veterans of Foreign Wars Post No. 3477, Athens, Ohio, no date.

Grandma's Pantry

Grandma's Pantry, the term used for the civil defense emergency food storage program, attracted women throughout the country. The newsletter, By, For, and About Women in Civil Defense, *explained the program. The newsletter was published in 1955 by the Federal Civil Defense Administration.*

GRANDMA'S PANTRY is creating a considerable interest all over the country, thanks to civil defense minded women.

As you probably have learned, GRANDMA'S PANTRY is the catch phrase for the civil defense emergency food storage program.

Borrowing an idea from Grandma's long years of experience in taking care of her family, the theme is: "Grandma's Pantry War Ready — Is Your Pantry Ready in Event of Emergency?"

Remember GRANDMA'S PANTRY with its shelves loaded with food, ready for any emergency, whether it be unexpected company or roads blocked for days by a winter's storm?

Today, as a result of the newly-created perils of possible enemy attack, GRANDMA'S PANTRY, or the re-creation of GRANDMA'S PANTRY in a sheltered area of the modern home, is once again a necessity.

In case of disaster — a flood, a tornado, or an enemy attack with mass destruction weapons — your home might be isolated, or food shipments to your community might be disrupted.

With a well-stocked pantry, you can be just as self-sufficient as Grandma was. Add a first aid kit, flashlight, and a portable radio to this supply, and you will have taken the first important step in civil defense preparedness for your country.

A minimum of seven days' supply of food and water or canned juices is recommended.

GRANDMA'S PANTRY originated in New York, caught hold in Maine where Inez Wing, Civil Defense Director of Women's Activities for the Maine Civil Defense agency, expanded the idea. Governor Cross proclaimed "Grandma's Pantry Week."

It jumped over to Portland where a sample GANDMA'S PANTRY was set up at a Food Fair, and now a number of states are planning for Pantry Booths to be featured at county fairs scheduled for the summer.

More and more women are getting behind GRANDMA'S PANTRY, with such groups as the Daughters of the American Revolution and the Veterans of Foreign Wars Auxiliary leading the way.

BY, FOR, AND ABOUT Women in Civil Defense

Mrs. Jean Wood Fuller
DIRECTOR OF WOMEN'S ACTIVITIES

GRANDMA'S PANTRY BELONGS IN YOUR KITCHEN

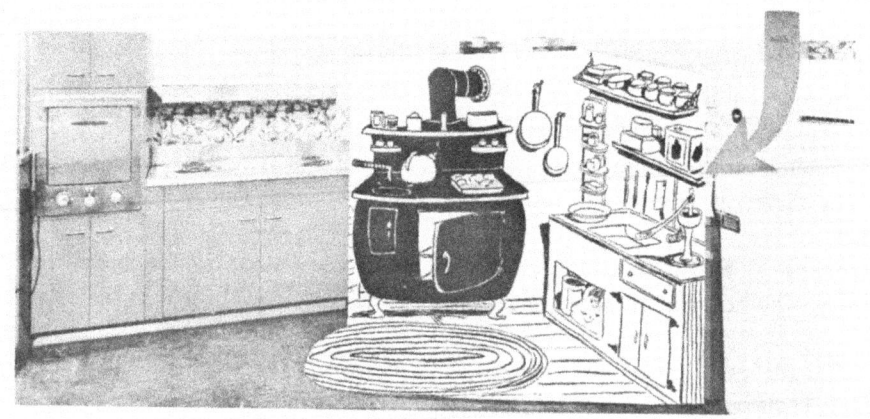

GRANDMA'S PANTRY AND HOW IT GREW

GRANDMA'S PANTRY is creating considerable interest all over the country, thanks to civil defense minded women.

As you probably have learned, GRANDMA'S PANTRY is the catch phrase for the civil defense emergency food storage program.

Borrowing an idea from Grandma's long years of experience in taking care of her family, the theme is: "Grandma's Pantry Was Ready - Is Your Pantry Ready in Event of Emergency?"

FEDERAL CIVIL DEFENSE ADMINISTRATION · BATTLE CREEK, MICHIGAN

Grandma's Pantry Belongs in Your Kitchen, Federal Civil Defense Administration, 1955.

What Should You Put Into a Modern Grandma's Pantry?

The following items have been suggested for your GRANDMA'S PANTRY. Remember, a three-day supply is the minimum, a week's supply would be preferable.

Select your own requirements in quantities suitable to your personal or family needs. Check "pantry" at least once a month and rotate regularly. Remember bottled water is important, and it must be changed every six weeks. Items packed in glass or other than tin should be wrapped in paper for protection against breakage or damage. Keep in dry storage. Home canned supplies are good items, too. All safety precautions should be taken for storage of cooking equipment using bottled gas or liquids.

Civil defense organizations across the country reprinted this illustration, as permitted by the Maine State Grocers Association, to encourage women to stock their Grandma's Pantry.

Canned Milk
Evaporated
Instant Non-fat Dry
Condensed

Canned Meats
Chicken
Fish
Meat Varieties
Stews
Bacon

Canned Soups
All Varieties
Chowders

Canned Fruit
All Varieties

Canned Vegetables
Potatoes
Peas
Baked Beans
String Beans
Corn
Tomatoes
Others

Canned Juices
Fruit and Vegetables

Beverages
Coffee
Tea
Cocoa
Water (Jugs)
Soft Drinks

Miscellaneous Needs
Flour — Also Prepared
Types
Dry Yeast
Sugar
Salt and Pepper
Soap and Powder

Paper Supplies	Can Opener	Honey
Toilet Tissues	Baby Foods	Jam
Safety Matches	Pet Foods	Spreads
Candles	Canned Heat	Dry Fruits
Kitchen Silver, etc.	Shortening	Cereals
First Aid Kits	Pails and Buckets	Brown Bread
Olive Oil	Crackers	

Home Defense Corps

Cities across the country initiated activities and organizations to promote civil defense. The Home Defense Corps in Milwaukee encouraged women to volunteer their services to promote the importance of civil defense before an attack. Your Civil Defense Manual: A Handbook on Personal Survival, *published by the Milwaukee Civil Defense Administration, describes the purpose of the Corps.*

A new civil defense unit has been setting records in Milwaukee since 1955. The unit has a name, active members, and a vitally important mission. It is the Home Defense Corps.

The Home Defense Corps is an organization of trained persons who have the mission of helping Milwaukee families and neighborhoods prepare adequate civil defense plans. Through the Corps, civil defense information can get into each home in Milwaukee through personal contact.

Public education in basic survival techniques is *the* most important phase of civil defense. An informed public will know how to act in an emergency, and the possibility of panic will be lessened. Because of the importance of pre-disaster information to the civil defense cause, Milwaukee Civil Defense Director Dan E. Carleton decided, in April, 1955, that an organization should be created that would deal *only* with the pre-disaster information problem. The Home Defense Corps was then established. Its mission again — to do the public education job of bringing civil defense into every home in Milwaukee.

The Home Defense Corps is made up of volunteers who serve as Home Defense staff personnel, instructors, or officers. A Home Defense officer has the all-important job of providing civil defense information and assistance to approximately 20 families in a neighborhood. An officer receives his training and information from Home Defense instructors who teach an eighteen-hour course, including six hours of teacher training at the Milwaukee Vocational and Adult schools.

Six hours of basic civil defense orientation, including the history of civil defense, atomic and hydrogen weapons, evacuation planning, shelter concepts, panic prevention, and the Milwaukee organization, are included in both the officer and instructor training. Also included are six hours of home defense practices, including the makeup and mission of the Corps, emergency home firefighting, sanitation measures, first aid, and other items, and a Home Defense officer workshop covering basic methods of approaching the neighborhood families.

Administrative control of the Corps is maintained through Home Defense sector

Your Civil Defense Manual: A Handbook on Personal Survival, Milwaukee Civil Defense Administration, no date.

directors of the eight Milwaukee evacuation sectors. Each sector is further divided into areas and public school districts with directors and district supervisors in charge of each. These sector and area directors and district supervisors are responsible for the Home Defense Corps recruitment, training, and administrative details within their geographical units.

Normally, Home Defense officer training is given in public, parochial, or private schools, churches, or clubrooms in a particular school district. Lesson plans, films, handouts, textbooks, and training aids are provided by the Milwaukee Civil Defense Administration.

On graduation, Home Defense personnel receive an attractive pin, certificate, civil defense decals, and an official identification card. A further phase of the Corps' incentive program includes the attendance of volunteer staff personnel at Federal Staff College courses in Battle Creek, Mich. The Corps stresses a five-point program to maintain volunteer interest and enthusiasm. This program includes active training, operations, social activities, incentive awards, and continuous, advanced training.

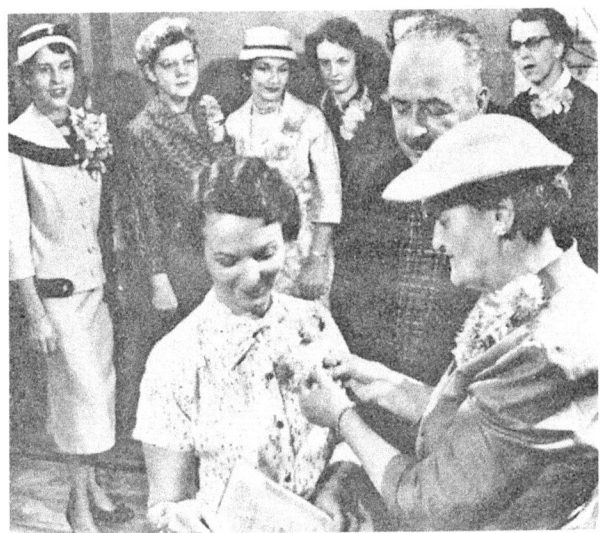

Top: Graduation ceremonies were held for each officer and instructor class. The class involved 18 hours of instruction, including six hours of teacher training. *Bottom:* Milwaukee's first officer class graduated 23. The ultimate goal to ensure adequate civil defense was 10,000 Home Defense officers and 400 instructors.

A survey count on Jan. 1, 1957, put the Corps' strength at 1,400 officers and 240 instructors. A goal of 10,000 Home Defense officers and 400 Home Defense instructors has been set for Milwaukee in order to accomplish the pre-disaster information job.

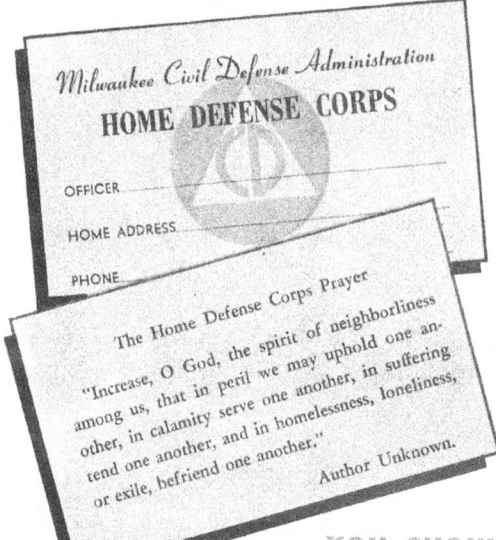

HOME DEFENSE *Can Help You* PREPARE NOW...

Civil defense preparedness includes all families in your neighborhood. Your neighborhood Home Defense officer will help you to develop a family civil defense plan.

If you have no Home Defense officer in your neighborhood, you should work with friends and neighbors to develop your district's civil defense plan.

It takes only a little time and effort for YOU to prepare your home and family against enemy attack.

...BEFORE DISASTER STRIKES

YOU SHOULD KNOW...

1. Evacuation route your family will use in time of emergency
2. Where your family will go
3. What the siren signals mean
4. How to tune in Conelrad (640–1240)
5. What foods to store and how to prepare them
6. Shelter requirements for your home
7. Emergency action to save lives
8. Firefighting and fire prevention
9. The four defenses against radioactive fallout
10. How to prevent panic in time of disaster

YOU SHOULD HAVE...

1. A family civil defense plan
2. A battery-powered radio with Conelrad markings
3. A portable, emergency Survival Kit with food for the family sufficient for one week
4. A prepared, stocked shelter area in your home
5. At least one member of the family trained in emergency first aid action and home nursing
6. At least one member of the family trained in basic civil defense orientation
7. The necessary equipment for home firefighting
8. Materials for emergency home sanitation
9. Your car's gas tank at least half full at all times
10. A first aid kit for your home and car

CONTACT YOUR HOME DEFENSE OFFICER *Today!*

Write to **CIVIL DEFENSE, MILWAUKEE 16**

Milwaukee's Home Defense Corps focused primarily on stay-at-home women with the time and energy to develop family civil defense plans with their friends and neighbors "before disaster strikes."

Medical Aides

After an atomic attack, thousands of people would need medical attention, with doctors and nurses in short supply and hospitals possibly destroyed. The answer for women in the State of New York was to become a medical aide, as described in "Operation Survival" and You, published in 1953 by the New York State Civil Defense Commission.

An atomic attack on one of our cities would result in the injury of tens of thousands of people — all needing immediate medical care. There will not be enough doctors, nurses, ambulances, or hospitals to care for all of them. Many will die needlessly unless medical forces in the attacked city, from nearby cities, and in distant cities, have been organized and trained to help.

The Emergency Medical Services of Civil Defense are planning the medical activities which must begin immediately after an atomic bombing. It is training tens of thousands of Medical Aides for their jobs in this service; for after attack there will be no time to learn what to do and how to do it....

When you complete your training, you will be prepared to help save the life of someone who may be injured in a peacetime accident. If we are attacked by our enemies, YOU WILL SAVE MANY LIVES.

Effects of the Atom Bomb

There is a blinding flash of light; a few seconds later, a tremendous blast. An atom bomb has exploded. In a few minutes thousands die and thousands more are dying or severely injured; buildings topple; fires rage; streets and cellars are flooded; live wires are exposed; gas mains break; and glass and rubble lie everywhere.

A bomb like the one exploded over Hiroshima will cause almost total destruction within a half-mile of the center of the explosion, called *Ground Zero*. From one-half to one mile, the damage is severe; to one and five-eighths miles, it is moderate. From this point up to eight miles from Ground Zero, the damage ranges from partial to light. If the bomb bursts high in the air, there remain no dangerous amounts of radioactivity on the ground. If the bomb is exploded underwater, the radiation danger is increased.

The largest number of seriously injured people are in the areas of severe damage. Half of the injured are suffering from burns, caused either by the intense heat of the bomb or by flames from burning buildings. Falling buildings, flying glass, and missiles have

"Operation Survival" and You, New York State Civil Defense Committee, 1953.

caused crushing injuries, fractures, and wounds. Many of the injured are in a state of severe shock. Some people who escaped injury from the bomb are hurt later by fires, floods, and collapsing buildings.

Civil Defense

Across the nation, great numbers of men and women have already joined Civil Defense. They are training and participating in test exercises, manning the Civil Defense services that will work together to save lives and restore our cities after an atomic attack. In addition to medical, these services include warden, fire, police, transport, rescue, radiological (determines dangers from nuclear radiation), welfare, communications, public works, and public information.

Strong local Civil Defense organizations are the backbone of our Civil Defense. However, the Federal Government encourages states to set up Civil Defense programs, furnishes part of the funds for supplies, and arranges for Civil Defense forces to come from other states to the aid of the bombed areas.

The state organizations, such as the New York State Civil Defense Commission, help and advise local organizations, and furnish supplies, plans, and training aids. Our State organization also arranges for aid to come to attacked cities.

Every community in the State is a part of a *local Civil Defense jurisdiction*, which has a *Civil Defense Director* for all services. (In some places, this local jurisdiction covers a whole county; in others, a single city.) Within each Civil Defense jurisdiction, Emergency Medical Services is headed by a Chief Medical Officer.

Certain of these jurisdictions are called *target areas*, because they are the most likely to be attacked. Since no city can survive after attack without outside aid, certain jurisdictions near target cities will act as *Automatic Aid* areas. This means that immediately following attack, Civil Defense workers in an Automatic Aid area go to their target city without waiting for specific orders. They furnish help without losing the time so essential to saving lives.

If their target city is not attacked, medical workers may go on State orders to a city that has been attacked; or they may help to care for injured who are sent to their communities from attacked cities.

We Are Preparing

The Emergency Medical Services is planning an "*Operation Survival*" that will come to life immediately after an atomic attack anywhere in the State.

Because of the large numbers of personnel, supplies, and equipment involved, each target city has been divided into *zones*, which are under the direction of a *Zone Commander*. Medical operations in each zone are directed by a *Zone Medical Officer*. The Zone Medical Officer assigns the medical workers and supplies to stations in his zone of the city. He directs the movement of patients out of the area, and he decides where medical stations should be set up. Medical installations within each zone are First Aid Stations,

Secondary Aid Stations, Improvised Emergency Hospitals, remaining permanent hospitals, and Holding Stations.

Buildings that can be used for secondary aid stations, holding stations, and improvised emergency hospitals have already been earmarked. First Aid Stations will be set up after attack where they are needed.

"Teams" of medical workers are being trained in all areas of the State to set up and operate these medical installations. Each medical "team" consists of one physician, one medical associate (dentist, veterinarian, medical student), three nurses, one supply officer (pharmacist), forty medical aides, one messenger leader, and eight messengers.

The duty of Medical Aides in the "field" (the devastated area) is to keep the injured person alive until he can be brought to medical care. In stations, Medical Aides help doctors and nurses to give medical care and to operate the station.

Training steps for Medical Aides consist of a first aid course, an aid station training course, and hospital or other advanced training.

During training, and after it is completed, all medical workers take part in periodic drills and test exercises, so that, if and when an atom bomb explodes, they will know *what* to do, *when* to do it, and *how* to work together.

Part 4

Be Prepared

If an Attack Occurs:

DON'T GET PANICKY—

Keep cool.

It may save your life.

If We Are Bombed: A Handbook for Protection, St. Paul (Minn.) Civil Defense, no date.

ACT NOW ON YOUR PATRIOTIC
HOME DEFENSE PLEDGE

REMEMBER THAT A TRAINED,
alert AMERICA
IS A MIGHTY FORCE FOR PEACE

What You Can Do Now! Federal Civil Defense Administration, no date.

Operation Alert

The Federal Civil Defense Administration instituted Operation Alert in 1954 as a drill to test the readiness of various government agencies in the event of nuclear attack. The drill began with a hypothetical attack on the nation's capital and other cities across the country. The government held Operation Alert each year through 1961. In April 1958, Innis D. Harris, an evaluation officer for the 1957 Operation Alert, presented the background leading up to the tests, as well as his most recent findings to the Industrial College of the Armed Forces.

Operation Alert, as I'm sure you know, is a name which has been used to identify integrated test exercises conducted by the Federal Government. The lessons learned from these exercises are in substance the sum total of our experience in mobilization planning to cope with any emergency — limited war and general war — but principal emphasis has been placed on situations involving a nuclear attack on the continental United States....

First, how these exercises got started. Historically, due to our geographical position, the speed of travel, the range and destructive power of weapons, little attention was given to mobilization planning in peacetime. We had time. Between World War I and World War II, the military had foreseen the need for mobilization planning in peacetime, to purchase the time needed in war. Extensive plans were developed, as you know, notably the Mobilization Plan of 1937. But the various agencies of Government that would be needed to put the plans into action did not participate in this planning; nor were they familiar with the plans. In the absence of this Government-wide participation, the benefit was largely lost in the rush and confusion of the "battle against time" which came with the sudden outbreak of hostilities at Pearl Harbor. From this we learned a lesson — the need for Government-wide participation in the development of plans. We also learned some lessons during World War II. We learned that the nature of warfare was changing rapidly, that weapons of mass destruction increasingly involve civilian populations, that the contraction of distances makes time increasingly precious, and that mobilization planning involves some degree of instant readiness. We learned that if there was to be an acceptable state of readiness, we must do in time of peace that which we would no longer have time to do after the commencement of hostilities.

Now, to capitalize on these lessons, the National Security Act was enacted in 1947. It provided for (1) a National Security Council to integrate domestic, foreign, and military policies; (2) a Central Intelligence Agency to coordinate the direction of intelligence activities; (3) a Department of Defense to provide coordinated direction for the military establishment; (4) the Joint Chiefs of Staff for the preparation of joint military war plans;

The Federal Civil Defense Administration used the "Mr. Civil Defense" illustration, created by Al Capp, in various publications, as well as on the 1956 poster promoting National Civil Defense Week.

and (5) a National Security Resources Board, now the Office of Defense Mobilization, for the coordination of military, industrial, and civilian mobilization plans.

Three years later, in 1950, came the Korean War; mobilization plans took second place to activities in support of the war we were then fighting. By 1953, the Korean War became stabilized. In August 1953, the USSR detonated a thermonuclear device. In October 1953, the President stated that the Soviets now have the capability of atomic attack on us, and such capability will increase with the passage of time. Increased emphasis was now to be placed on adjusting our mobilization preparedness measures to the possibility of nuclear warfare.

A few months later, early in 1954, after some review of the continental United States defense posture, following the study that was made by the Bull committee and presented to the National Security Council, the President was presented with what was called a mobilization plan. It was a feeble plan by comparison with current concepts. In fact, there may be some question as to whether or not it was a plan in the true sense of the word. It was in the nature of a checklist of Policy actions. I might say it was an abbreviated form of the British War Book.

The President's reaction to the plan was this: No plan is any better than it works. Test it. And that is how we got started on test exercises — an activity entirely new to the Federal Government. We were faced with many novel questions: How could a mobilization plan be tested? What should be the objectives of a test? What should be its scope? Who should participate? What assumptions should be used as to the possible situations we would face? How realistic should it be?

In 1954, a few high-level officials, assuming several hours warning of a hypothetical attack, left Washington with a checklist of possible actions. They assembled in a cave. Water was dripping from the ceiling and oozing from the walls. This was the setting for our first exercise. The exercise lasted only a few hours, but a great deal was learned, believe it or not. The participants needed information on the attack situation to determine what policies were actually necessary. They didn't have it. They needed assistance in the preparation of documents to reflect policy decisions. They didn't have it. They needed to communicate policy directives to the departments and agencies concerned. They couldn't do it. They needed to know that the agencies had a capability to carry out the policy directives if they could issue them. They had no way of knowing. So a new push was given to the development of physical features for carrying on government — relocation sites, an interagency communication system, and the further development of plans.

We now have some 90 relocation sites in the seat of Government arc from 30 to 300 miles of Washington, and over 300 relocation sites throughout the country for regional and field offices. The arc is connected with an interagency communication system, which is reasonably adequate and is in the process of further development. A few highly secure relocation sites for central direction and for the protection of central communications have either been constructed or are under construction. That's just a side note to show what development there has been in some of these things which seemed so dismal in 1954.

In 1957 a still more ambitious exercise was undertaken. As in 1956, it was a three-way exercise (that is, mobilization, civil defense, and military) at all levels. But, in addition, it was divided into three phases, which covered approximately six weeks. The first phase dealt with increasing international tensions, followed by limited war. The second phase dealt with a nuclear attack on the United States. The magnitude of the attack and the resulting problems can be deduced from an estimated number of casualties over twice that of 1956. Approximately half of the casualties were due to residual radiation. The third phase dealt with the post-attack situation, in which the management of surviving resources for winning the war and restoring the Nation became the Government's chief concern.

The exercise was participated in by approximately 13,000 Federal employees, and — get this — over half a million others, including military, State, local, and industrial personnel. Perhaps the most significant feature of the exercise was that it forced an integration of our two major mobilization plans: one for dealing with a situation short of general war, and the other for dealing with a surprise attack without the strategic warning which preliminary hostilities might give us. During the process of this integration in the exercise, one question became paramount, namely, what can be done, or what should have been done, in periods of international tension and limited war to make the Nation better prepared to meet the requirements of general war? In other words, if we get into a limited war situation, let's formulate our policies to support the limited war, but at the same time do it in a way, if possible, that will better prepare us in the event that the limited war develops into an attack situation. The magnitude of the attack and the growing implications of radioactive fallout required, I would say, almost a complete reappraisal of policies and the means for carrying them out.

Administrative facilities for dealing with an emergency had improved appreciably since 1956. Thirty-seven percent of the agencies rated themselves as being in a high state of readiness. Forty-five percent rated themselves as generally satisfactory, and only 18 percent indicated that there was need for considerable improvement. You might question these self-evaluations as being overly optimistic, but there is some justification for them. The increased year-round participation in mobilization planning activities over a period of four years was beginning to pay dividends. It should be credited for the extensive follow-through on Presidential decisions at various echelons, including field organization, and the high degree of confidence displayed in coping with a grave emergency. It should also be credited with the growing capability — and this is significant — to identify remaining deficiencies and unresolved problems. It takes competence to recognize a problem and a deficiency when you see them. Therefore, at the conclusion of Operation Alert 1957, due in part to the increased competence of participants, we found an increased number of deficiencies. The lessons learned in 1957 can be summarized best by citing some of the matters identified as needing particular attention.

1. Local planning and action — You've got to have something more than a seat of government and a headquarters to deal with an emergency situation. Many things — most things actually — have to be carried out at the local level. Greater emphasis must be placed on planning and action at the local level. To avoid placing unwarranted reliance on the regional and central machinery of the Federal Government, efforts must be made to utilize to the maximum local governmental authority, services, and resources, together with State controls, leadership, and persuasion.

Measures must be developed to assure a continuity of State and local governments, and to assure the maintenance of law and order, even by the use of extreme means, including martial law, insofar as necessary. Special guidance should be provided to local, State, and Federal field officials so as to enable them to take the appropriate actions during mobilization, attack, and recovery. Methods of communicating effectively among these officials, including a system for rapid record and telephone communications, must be developed.

2. Transportation is a matter needing attention. Steps must be taken to establish local control centers for transportation — it can't be done from headquarters — in order to

achieve the widest possible decentralization of transport control. Provision must be made for the continuity of district offices which handle railroad embargoes and priorities. Incidentally, practically every district railroad control office in the country was wiped out in the attack. Most of them, as you know, are located in major cities.

3. Communication — Governmental communications facilities require strengthening, particularly in the field. Arrangements should be worked out for the pooled utilization of message centers outside of damaged areas. The time lag between actions taken by the President and the distribution of the resulting documents to the agencies must be reduced. This involves standby and self-triggering orders which will reduce communication requirements.

4. Attack warning systems — Alternate warning systems should be developed which will become operative in the event that the main system suffers damage from an initial attack.

5. Regional structure — A common and consistent pattern of regional boundaries for purposes of an emergency should again be considered to make for greater efficiency and better coordination at the regional and local levels. Incidentally, there are some 17 departments and agencies with field offices and activities. As you know, there are six Army areas. At the time of the exercise in 1957, ODM had 10 regions, FCDA had 7 regions, and the other 15 departments and agencies had various field organizations with various boundaries. Now we are about to see the light of day when we will have among all the civilian agencies contiguous boundaries of regions for emergency administration. It appears that there may be eight, but well adjusted to the boundaries of the six Army areas.

6. Organizational problems — More extensive planning is needed for timing the establishment of emergency agencies — both pre-attack and post-attack — and coordinating their activities with the regular agencies. Questions were raised about the desirability of creating these emergency agencies in an attack situation. Can we afford to go through a reorganization at a time like that? Can we afford not to know where critical functions and responsibilities are scattered? Take transportation, for example. If such functions should be brought together, and if it is too difficult to do so post-attack, should it not be done now?

The scattering of responsibilities for health services among the Federal Civil Defense Administration; the Department of Health, Education, and Welfare; the Office of Defense Mobilization; and the Department of Labor should be reexamined. Organizational arrangements for handling domestic information, and for coordinating foreign information and propaganda activities need to be established now, at least on a ready basis, for wartime use. The existing list of essential wartime functions requires complete review to bring it up-to-date in view of the changing possible post-attack situations, as to what is essential and what isn't. Consideration should be given to limiting the number of delegations of requisitioning authority. There are too many agencies with authority to requisition the same property.

7. Central programming — Further study needs to be given to the central programming function as a means of dealing with the immediate post-attack problems, in addition to providing policy guidelines pre-attack for use in the event of attack. Central programming for the post-attack period must give principal attention to the management of surviving resources, taking account of losses and the possibility of long-term denial of

areas due to radiation, for the primary purpose of making the best immediate and potential use of what remains. The identification of the most limiting resource is essential to the formulation of meaningful central programs. The extreme limiting effects of the hypothetical fallout situation on manpower utilization emphasized the need to reexamine ways and means for the mobilization and utilization of trained manpower. The development of better mechanisms for the adjudication of conflicting claims on scarce resources is needed.

8. Production statistics — We have the know-how, the statistical tools, for handling the traditional job of mobilizing military (hard goods) production. This might be pretty obsolete if we are depending on military forces being in an attack situation, but we are not equipped with the statistical tools to mobilize critical items for human survival, under attack and post-attack conditions.

9. Damage assessment — Further study is needed of the capabilities of bomb damage assessment to provide prompt and adequate information for policy decisions, with emphasis on what survives rather than what is destroyed, emphasis on the "vertical" effects of production losses, and the quick identification of the overall most limiting factor on the utilization of total resources.

In addition to perfecting an electronic computation system for rapid assessment, work should begin on the development of on-the-ground surveys by technically competent people. Capabilities in radiological monitoring at the local level must be substantially improved. Incidentally, I think that we have moved very far in this field of electric computers, standby computers, here and there throughout the country.

10. Civilian survival stockpile and shelter programs — Approximately 50 percent of the hypothetical casualties occurred through lack of shelter and lack of critical survival items. Dealing with stockpile and shelter programs has to be on a long-term basis, rather than on an emergency basis, during a period of mobilization, when time may not be available to complete crash programs and when other mobilization demands of the Nation's resources are rapidly increasing.

11. Fallout — In addition to the hardening of sites against fallout, adequate equipment must be provided for fallout detection at relocation sites, and, for that matter, over the country as well.

12. Domestic economic policy — We had some of the same domestic economic policy problems that we had in previous years, i.e., establishing consistent policies among the Federal agencies. It now becomes clear that Federal, State, and local economic policies must also be made consistent.

13. Foreign economic policy — We had problems also with respect to foreign economic policy — economic warfare and foreign assistance. We need to improve our mechanisms for administering economic warfare measures. We need to study the means and capabilities for providing assistance to our allies and other friendly nations in relation to probable domestic needs. We need better and more integrated planning in the mobilization field between Canada and the United States. Incidentally, joint United States-Canadian participation in these exercises would be helpful.

14. Finally, the policy problems — The exercise demonstrated once again that a brief re-location period does not afford the time necessary for an adequate consideration of policy problems. Attention to such matters must be continuous, and a part of each agency's

normal work programs, to assure thorough staff consideration of documents, careful determination of requirements, and organizational responses to planned actions.

In summary, then, with respect to all exercises and all of the lessons learned, I think that the most lasting dividend is that we are developing throughout Government habits of thinking and the ability to react quickly to a new kind of emergency situation with which no government has had to deal. Our hope is, that if we are sufficiently prepared for such a situation, no one will ever have to deal with it. These exercises will not permit us to become complacent. There will never be a "plan" not subject to change, nor a document which cannot be modified. Each year, we must work against the problem of a dynamic situation. Each year, we improve plans, skills, and readiness.

CONELRAD

As part of the government's increasing response to and concerns about the Soviet Union's atomic threat, President Harry S Truman established CONELRAD *in 1951, an emergency service to be used in case of attack. The Federal Civil Defense Administration's brochure,* In Case of Attack! *explained how the system worked.*

Why should you tune to 640 or 1240 on your AM?
Because they are the only dial settings where you will receive authoritative civil defense information.

The broadcasting industry and the government, working together, have devised a special system of AM (Standard) radio broadcasting to bring you official information in time of emergency.

The system is officially called "Plan for CONtrol of ELectromagnetic RADiation"—CONELRAD for short.

Remember that name, CONELRAD. Remember what it means—"Tune your AM (Standard) radio to either 640 or 1240."

Under the CONELRAD emergency broadcasting system, you will be able to receive radio programs from three different sources—local, State, and National. Programs originating locally will be broadcast direct. Line connections are arranged for programs originating on a State or regional basis. By using the existing network structures and line connections between stations, defense officials can broadcast programs which will reach the entire country.

What else should you know about CONELRAD?
First, CONELRAD is the only safe broadcasting system yet devised to keep you informed of important civil defense news and instructions without helping enemy bombers reach their targets.

Second, CONELRAD may affect your radio listening habits in three ways:
1. CONTINUOUS METHOD: If you are in or near a large city, you will hear a continuous program of civil defense instructions and reports at 640 or 1240 kilocycles, or both, during the CONELRAD radio operation.
2. ON-OFF METHOD: In some smaller communities, your local radio station, operating at either 640 or 1240 kilocycles, will be on the air for some seconds, off the air for some minutes, on the air again, and off the air again in this continuing pattern until the end of the Alert.

3. NO BROADCAST: Unfortunately, CONELRAD cannot guarantee civil defense broadcasts for everyone because of technical limitations. Due to the reduction in transmitting power, a few parts of the country which normally receive AM (Standard) radio broadcasts may no longer be able to hear the diminished signal. Your radio *may* be silent, though experts are working to prevent this possibility.

Which number (640 or 1240) is the right one for your city?

Every effort will be made to tell you long in advance which AM frequency (640 or 1240) will be used in your community. In most large cities, both frequencies will be used. If you do not know which to rely on, tune from one of these dial settings to the other until the broadcast comes in.

Do not be alarmed if you receive no information for a brief period after the radio Alert has been announced. It takes a little time to switch from regular broadcasting to the special CONELRAD system. Wait a few minutes and then try 640 or 1240 again, whichever is designated for your area.

Suppose the signal "fades" ... is sometimes strong and sometimes weak.—Does that mean anything?

Yes, it does. When the CONELRAD continuous method is in operation, all stations in a community are required to reduce power and to broadcast a common program. Each station is on the air for only a few seconds at a time. Then another local station picks up as the other leaves off. You will hear a single program, but it is coming to you from a number of different stations—some of which are nearer to you than the others.

This may cause a signal that is sometimes weak and sometimes strong. If this happens, turn the volume up to the point where you can hear plainly, even though it may occasionally be quite loud.

In Case of Attack! Federal Civil Defense Administration, 1951.

If some communities use 640 and others use 1240, how will you know that you are tuned to the official civil defense broadcast for your city?

Find out as soon as possible from your local civil defense office or radio station which frequency will be used in your community. Then mark it permanently on your AM (Standard) radio dial, so you will always know the correct setting. In order not to help the enemy, there will be no station identification in an emergency. Even if you are tuned to another city, however, it will be one quite near to you and the news and information should be helpful.

How will you know when the emergency system of radio broadcasting is going into effect?

If you are listening to any kind of radio or television set when the Alert sounds, you will hear a message like this:

> "We interrupt our normal program to cooperate in security and civil defense measures as requested by the United States Government.... This is a CONELRAD radio Alert ... Listen carefully! This station is now leaving the air. During the CONELRAD radio Alert there will be no FM or TV programs. The only program on the air will be on your standard radio at 640 or 1240 kilocycles, starting in a few minutes. Tune your standard radio receiver to 640 or 1240 kilocycles for official instructions, news, and official information."

If you are not listening to your radio or TV set when this announcement is made, when you hear the civil defense sirens or attack warning signals, you will know that the CONELRAD system has gone into operation. Tune your AM (Standard) radio at once to the proper dial setting — 640 or 1240.

What kind of radio should you have for receiving official information?

As long as the flow of electric power is uninterrupted, your regular AM (Standard) radio set will do the job.

However, a battery-operated or portable radio is your best insurance that you will continue to receive official civil defense news and instructions even if local power fails. If you possibly can, have such a radio in your shelter area.

Your automobile radio will be a useful auxiliary set. Auto radios are battery operated. Unless your car is damaged or not operating, you can count on your car radio for receiving official civil defense information via the CONELRAD system.

But even the best radios aren't much help if you and all members of your family don't know where to tune in or haven't marked the dial setting with the CONELRAD NUMBERS — 640 or 1240.

Who gives the signal for CONELRAD to start and stop?

The Air Defense Command, U.S. Air Force, will order the attack warning which will activate the CONELRAD system. AM (Standard) radio stations will switch, in a matter of minutes, to the emergency broadcasting system on one of the two officially designated CD frequencies — 640 or 1240 kilocycles (marked as 64 or 124 on most radio dials).

The Air Defense Command, U.S. Air Force, also determines when it is safe for radio to resume normal broadcasting following the radio Alert.

IF YOU HAVE HAD NO WARNING IN AN A-BOMB ATTACK

WHEN YOU SEE A FLASH OF LIGHT BRIGHTER THAN THE SUN —

- Don't run: there isn't time.
- Fall flat on your face.
- **GET DOWN FAST!**

Above and opposite: Protection from the Atomic Bomb. Civil Defense Agency of the Commonwealth of Massachusetts, 1950.

IF OUT-OF-DOORS

GET DOWN!

Drop to the ground: close against a wall if possible.

Cover up.

Stay down until the blast has passed; then get under the heaviest cover nearby.

STAY THERE FOR AT LEAST A MINUTE

IF IN YOUR CAR

Stop the car fast, set the emergency brake, and dive for the floor.

STAY DOWN FOR AT LEAST A MINUTE

•

IF YOU HAVE NO AIR-RAID WARNING

WHEN YOU SEE THE FLASH
THERE IS NO TIME TO RUN

WHEREVER YOU ARE GET DOWN FAST

Look to the Sky

The Ground Observer Corps (GOC) began during World War II, with more than a million civilian volunteers manning 14,000 observation posts along the nation's coasts. In February 1950, General Ennis Whitehead of the Continental Air Command proposed the formation of a new GOC with 160,000 volunteers operating 8,000 observation posts located in gaps between radar network sites. The revised GOC plan, called "Operation SKYWATCH," began on July 14, 1952. At its peak, more than 800,000 civilian volunteers, young and old, watched for an enemy attack at some 16,000 observation posts across the country. The GOC ended in 1959. One Call: The Ground Observer Corps, published in the early 1950s, explained the life-and-death importance of volunteering.

The Threat

In the event of World War *III*, we must assume that the Soviet Union will strike first — and hard!

The Reds will try to knock us out in a single blow.
If we are to survive — prevent a surprise atom bomb attack — we must have warning!
You can be an important figure in our warning systems.

The Facts

TODAY

... the Soviet Union has more than 1,000 long-range bombers in the Red Air Force. *For what purpose?*

TODAY

... the Reds have enough bombs to inflict a devastating blow against the most vital targets in the United States in a single day. No part of the nation is safe from the threat of these bombs — dropped by accident or by design.

> IF WE ARE TO SURVIVE
> WE MUST HAVE WARNING
> WE MUST HAVE WARNING
> IF WE ARE TO SURVIVE

Are We the Target?

TODAY

The Soviet Union has polar bases from which their long-range bombers could fly to any part of the United States in a matter of hours. These bases are useful to the Red Air Force *only* for an attack against us!

What About Our Present Warning System?

TODAY

... our warning system consists of two factors — Radar and Civilian Plane Spotters in the Ground Observer Corps.

Radar — This electronic device is in operation 24 hours a day, but there are dangerous, unavoidable gaps in our present system through which low-flying enemy aircraft could sneak undetected.

Plane Spotters — The volunteer civilian plane spotter *can* fill the gaps in our radar network, but there are too few of them at the present time to do the job adequately. The thousands of patriotic citizens now in the Ground Observer Corps need and deserve your help in the defense of our country. *With one* telephone call, one spotter could start the warning that might save a city. *You* could be the one to make that call.

ONE CALL

One call from a civilian plane spotter could sound the alarm that would give our interceptor pilots in the Air Defense Command more time to challenge the invaders in the sky *before they reached their targets*.

One call could alert the Army Anti-Aircraft batteries in time to swing into action.

One call might save our long-range bombers in the Strategic Air Command from possible destruction on the ground — give them a chance to strike back at the enemy in his own territory.

One Call: Ground Observer Corps, U.S. Air Force, circa 1952.

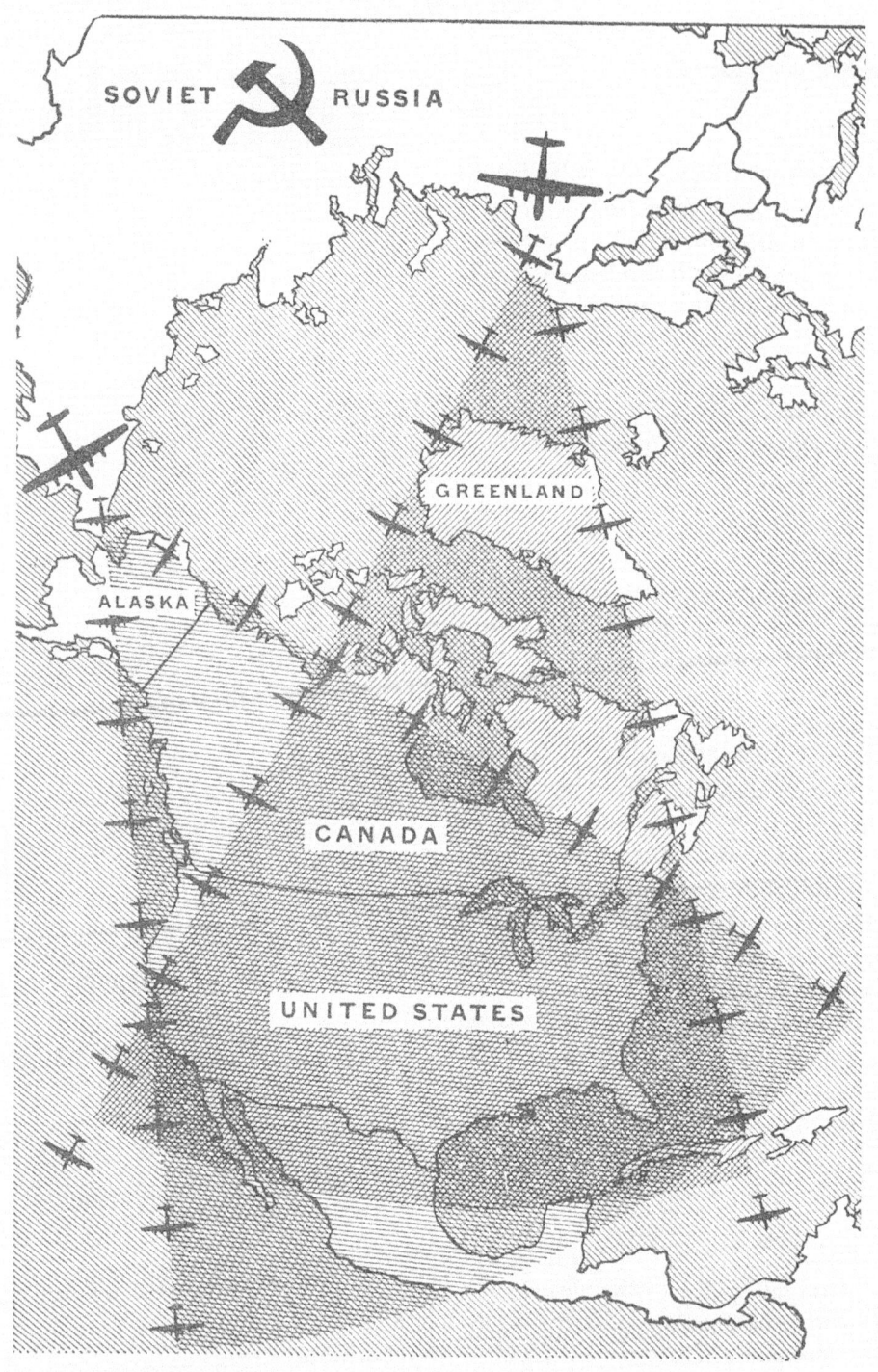

As this map from the *One Call* pamphlet illustrated, the Soviet Union's polar air bases meant it could launch an atomic attack with long-range bombers and hit virtually anywhere in the United States within hours. This probability made the Ground Observer Corps an essential part of the nation's civil defense plans.

One call could give local Civil Defense organizations more time to sound the air raid warning.

You could make that one all-important call as a Civilian Plane Spotter if the Red bombers ever come.

Learning to Be a Spotter Is Not Difficult

You don't have to be an expert at identifying airplanes to become a useful Civilian Plane Spotter.

Any intelligent person with normal sight or hearing can learn to be an important figure in our warning system after two or three simple lessons.

You are only asked to report the flight of aircraft in your area of observation — their approximate number — approximate height — and approximate direction of flight.

A typical call to your nearest Air Defense Filter Center goes like this: "Aircraft Flash!" When you are connected with the Filter Center, you identify your observation post by some code name such as "Gopher reporting — two multimotored planes — flying very low — direction South." etc.

You are asked to work usually only two hours a week with other volunteers in an observation post near your home.

The job of the observer is not easy — it is not exciting — but some day it could be the most important job of your whole life.

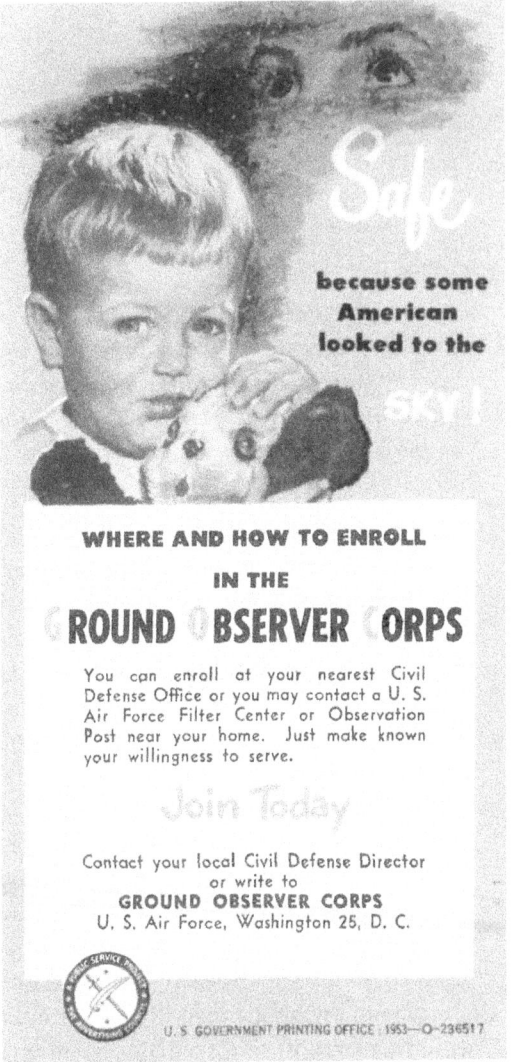

Women — or, more specifically, stay-at-home mothers — were considered vital to America's civil defense efforts, including the Ground Observer Corps. This was never more evident than in this image of a mother's eyes above a small boy, with the caption, "Safe because some Americans looked to the SKY!" (*The Time for Air Defense Is Now!*, 1953.)

Plane Spotters

American youth played a key role in the Ground Observer Program. Junior and high school students from around the country—from major cities to small towns—participated as aircraft or plane spotters. Schools encouraged students to volunteer their time to help guard against an atomic attack. Civil Defense Manual for Georgia Schools, *published in 1952, describes to teachers how the program works and its importance.*

Students of the Junior and Senior grades in the High Schools of the State of Georgia will find training and performance as "aircraft spotters" for the Ground Observer Corps Program to be a most interesting project. In addition to the point of interest, members participating will be rendering a great and noble service to their country's defenses. Conditions in the world today make the Ground Observer Corps an absolute necessity. We do not know when or where we might be attacked by enemy aircraft.

It is suggested that groups either formal or informal be organized for the purpose of training together for positions as observers for Ground Observer Posts, or if in the cities of Atlanta or Savannah, as plotters, tellers, and filterers for the Filter Centers. These can be in the form of Aircraft Spotter Clubs or some other designation. Assistance and training for these groups can be arranged through the Office of The Air Force Coordinator, Ground Observer Corps, Georgia Department of Civil Defense, 959 Confederate Avenue S.E., Atlanta. Because of the number of posts now under organization, and their location eight miles apart, every interested student can be assured of an opportunity to participate in the program. Within a few miles of every home in the State of Georgia, there will be a Ground Observer Post that will eventually have to be manned 24 hours around the clock!

The purpose of the Corps is to fill in all the blind spots of the radar screen—that portion of the area that comes under the line of sight capabilities of radar. Blind spots are caused by the topography of the terrain. Only those points designated will take part in the Ground Observer Corps.

The Corps provide information to our Air Defense Control Centers via a very simple system. First, a civilian volunteer reports by telephone from his assigned observation post, all the aircraft he sees or hears. Secondly, a Filter Center takes the information from the observers, establishes the speed and direction of the airplanes, which means that they have established a track, and passes the information on to the Air Defense Control Center.

Filter Centers are located in cities best equipped for prompt reception of the observers'

Junior and high school students in the 1950s could choose from a wide array of clubs and organizations, including Aircraft Spotter Clubs associated with the Ground Observer Corps. For their efforts, students received the GOC pin, shown in the illustration, and the knowledge that they helped to protect the country from a sneak attack.

telephone calls. The Filter Center is also manned by civilian volunteers. A typical Filter Center occupies a large room containing a horizontal plotting board on which the aircraft traffic is plotted, and a platform surrounding that board on which tellers pass the plotted information on to other Filter Centers and Air Force stations.

The actual organizations and recruiting of the Ground Observer Corps is the responsibility of the Georgia Department of Civil Defense. Training is carried out by the United States Air Force with mobile training teams located at each Filter Center. The Air Force has assigned an Officer to each state organizing the Ground Observer Corps within their borders for the express purpose of coordination.

What to Do If You're Bombed

If the Niagara Frontier is BOMBED, published in 1950 by the Niagara Frontier Civil Defense Offices, is an early example of government-sponsored brochures designed to explain what to do in case of an atomic attack.

The purpose of this booklet is to help you answer the question: "*What do I do if an atomic bomb is dropped?*"

As terrible as the bomb is, it will not spread as much death as many people think — [or] mean the end of our great cities, our state, our nation.

Certainly we must face the fact that at the center of the explosion thousands of lives will be lost, and an entire large city could be crippled temporarily by one bomb.

There is no complete defense against an atomic bomb, but, by careful CIVIL DEFENSE planning, NOW, and by full understanding on your part of what you can do NOW and what you should do in time of disaster, the effects of the bomb can be greatly minimized.

In case of attack, the enemy will probably concentrate on areas of dense population and industry. The people of the so-called "safe areas" must be ready to help those who might be bombed. What you should do in time of attack are simple things — but ALL-IMPORTANT.

Lucius D. Clay, Chairman,
New York State Civil Defense Commission

What to Do in an Air Attack

A radar network and a force of volunteer airplane spotters is being established to detect a possible enemy attack. If enemy raiders are spotted, an air raid siren will be sounded. Your local Civil Defense Office has established a control center with a direct wire to the Key Air Raid Warning Center, which is manned 24 hours a day, 7 days a week, and the local sirens will be sounded within seconds after the first alarm is received.

But we also must consider the possibility that the enemy will be able to evade our defenses and deliver a bomb before a warning can be sounded.

If the Niagara Frontier Is Bombed, Niagara (N.Y.) Frontier Civil Defense Offices, no date.

Sneak Attack

In case of a sneak attack, there are several things you can do to protect yourself, even though you may not be able to reach shelter.

The blinding flash will be your first warning. If you are in the open, immediately fall to the ground face down next to a building wall, if possible, so you will be shielded from falling brick and stones. Cover your face, neck and arms. Close your eyes. This will give you some protection against the deadly radiation and scorching heat. If you are on the street, dodge into a doorway, if it is not more than a step or two away. Stand to one side under the arch of a door. Turn away from the flash and cover your face and other exposed parts of your body.

If you are in the house, throw yourself on the floor next to the outside wall. Or better, crawl under a bed or table, or drop behind a sofa or any other large object which can protect you from flying glass or falling plaster. Keep out of line with windows. Cover up.

Air Raid Warnings

WHEN THE ENEMY ATTACK IS BELIEVED TO BE IMMINENT, THE SIRENS WILL BLOW A RISING AND FALLING SIGNAL FOR THREE MINUTES. This is the only warning you will receive and you must act immediately, but do not become panicky. You can save yourself.

An attacking plane may fly over many towns and cities before reaching its target. All these cities will be warned. The Air Raid warning does not necessarily mean that your city is the target, but remember, the undulating siren means TROUBLE somewhere near. TAKE COVER. Unless announced in advance as a TEST, the AIR RAID SIREN MEANS BUSINESS.

When You Hear the Siren

Know your designated shelter. Get down into it or into the basement as fast as you can without pushing people around. Take cover, but be SENSIBLE. Don't be panicky.

Blast is most destructive to the upper floors of buildings. If you can't get downstairs, get into the center hall, the core of the structure.

If you cannot get out of your office or apartment in time: Get under a desk or heavy table, if possible lie close to the wall where you are not in line with the windows. Cover your neck, head, and arms with your coat. Close your eyes tightly. These precautions will help protect you from flying glass or debris, as well as the heat and radiation from the explosion.

If you are on the street: Get to the nearest shelter or basement. If none are available, step into the nearest doorway or into the lobby of any concrete building. Face away from the street and from windows. Pull your coat over your head or shield your head with your arms if without coat.

If you are driving a car: Park at the curb as quickly as you can. Don't park where you will block traffic. Leave your keys in the car. Get out and seek shelter at once.

What to Do if You're Bombed

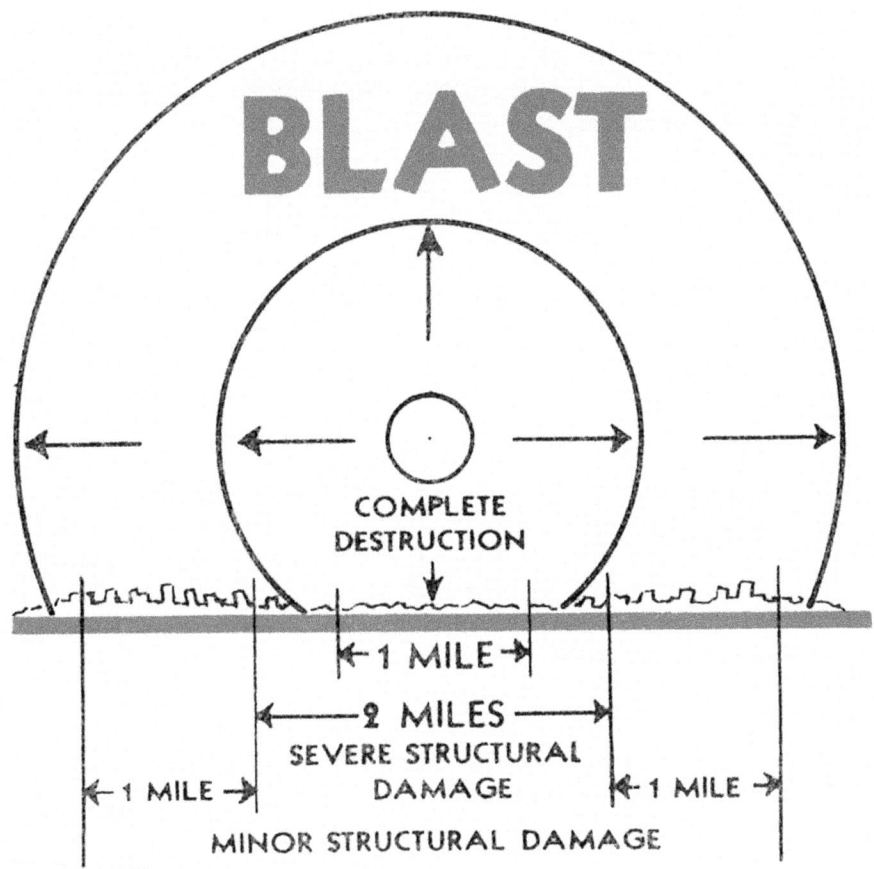

As shown in this illustration, anyone unfortunate enough to be within a mile of the blast did not have a chance of survival.

If you live in a frame house: Shut off oil burner, put out fire in fireplaces, turn off electric heaters, stove, and other appliances. If you care to do so, you may turn off electricity and gas at the meter. Close all doors and windows. Draw curtains and blinds. Extinguish coal fires in stoves and furnaces. Get into the basement if you have one. If you do not have a basement, your neighbor who has a good basement will have room for you. Take a flashlight, and a supply of warm clothing if it is winter. (Survey has been made by your AIR RAID WARDEN, and he has a list of neighborhood basements available.)

Have several buckets of SAND and WATER and a FIRST AID KIT handy.

The All Clear

When an enemy plane has been shot down or has passed by without attack or has made its attack and has departed, the sirens will blow an ALL CLEAR, a series of three one-minute steady blasts separated by two minutes of silence.

The immediate effect of the explosion will be over in a few seconds, BUT BEFORE YOU GO OUT, WAIT A FEW MINUTES FOR THE ALL CLEAR SIGNAL. LOOK

OUT for falling debris. Don't RUN AWAY AND LEAVE EVEN A SMALL FIRE BURNING. If, because of fire or damage, you must leave the house and there are clouds of dust or spray outside, cover your mouth and nose with handkerchief or cloth. The dust, if from wrecking, may be harmless, but BE CAREFUL; A GROUND OR WATER BURST may have spread radioactive dirt or fog through the air. If you are not in an area of serious damage, stay indoors and keep the windows closed.

Once the raiders are clear, change your clothes and bathe. Scrub hard and use plenty of SOAP. Be careful to get your hair and fingernails CLEAN.

Here is a summary of the most important things to remember in case of an atomic attack.

What You Should Do

Keep calm.

If there is time, get to shelter at once.

If no underground shelter is close by, get into the ground floor of a nearby building or even stand in a doorway if nothing better is available.

If you see the bomb flash and there is no cover of any kind within a step or two, drop to the street or gutter, turn away from flash, and close eyes tightly. Cover head, face, neck, arms, and other exposed areas of the body.

If you are indoors, turn off appliances such as electric toasters, irons, stoves, etc. Get into the core of your building and under a desk or table if there isn't time to get to the basement. Lie face downward and out of line with windows. After the burst, tie handkerchief over mouth if area is contaminated.

What You Should Not Do

Don't telephone.

Don't turn on water after blast, unless to fight fire.

Don't eat or drink in a contaminated area.

Don't use metal goods in a contaminated area.

Don't touch things after ground or water burst.

Don't try to drive your car.

Don't get excited or excite others.

Don't spread rumors.

What you should do *NOW!* to save a life, possibly your own

1. Enlist in your local CIVIL DEFENSE Program.
2. Take a course in FIRST AID.
3. Eliminate fire hazards in your home or shop.
   Clean out rubbish in attic and cellar.
   Provide a clear area in basement for shelter and equip it with FIRST AID KIT, a couple pails of sand and water, flashlight, and shovel.
   A stirrup pump is highly recommended. With it, a little water will do the most good.

What to Do if You're Bombed 99

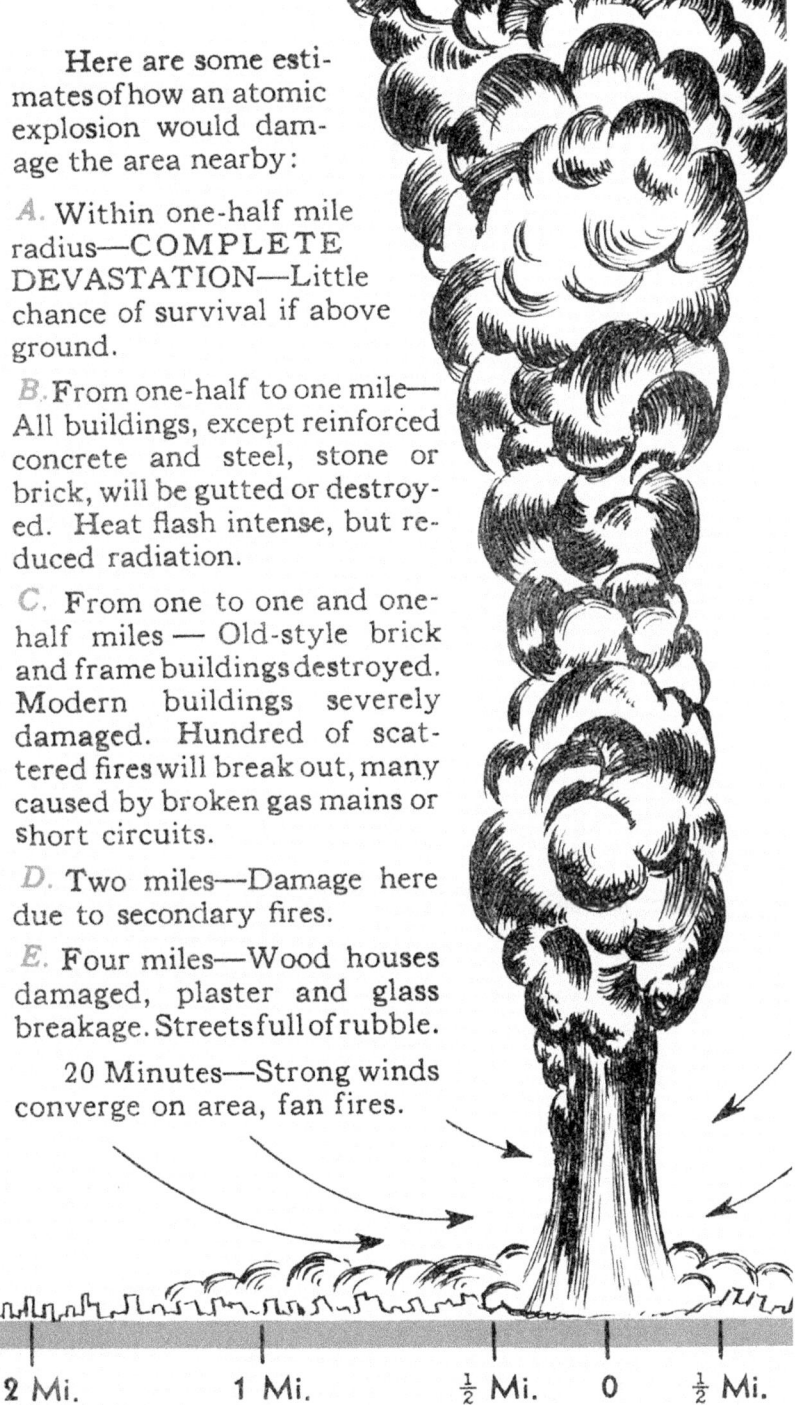

Here are some estimates of how an atomic explosion would damage the area nearby:

A. Within one-half mile radius—COMPLETE DEVASTATION—Little chance of survival if above ground.

B. From one-half to one mile—All buildings, except reinforced concrete and steel, stone or brick, will be gutted or destroyed. Heat flash intense, but reduced radiation.

C. From one to one and one-half miles — Old-style brick and frame buildings destroyed. Modern buildings severely damaged. Hundred of scattered fires will break out, many caused by broken gas mains or short circuits.

D. Two miles—Damage here due to secondary fires.

E. Four miles—Wood houses damaged, plaster and glass breakage. Streets full of rubble.

20 Minutes—Strong winds converge on area, fan fires.

2 Mi.   1 Mi.   ½ Mi.   0   ½ Mi.

Americans needed to know their best options for surviving an atomic explosion, including the type of buildings most likely to withstand the blast and heat. As shown here, these buildings included reinforced concrete, steel, stone, and brick.

Before and During an Atomic Attack

Local, state, and federal government publications stressed the importance of being prepared at all times and for every situation. Just in Case Atom Bombs Fall, *published in 1951 by the Civil Defense Office of Denver, provided step-by-step guidelines for what to do before and during an atomic attack.*

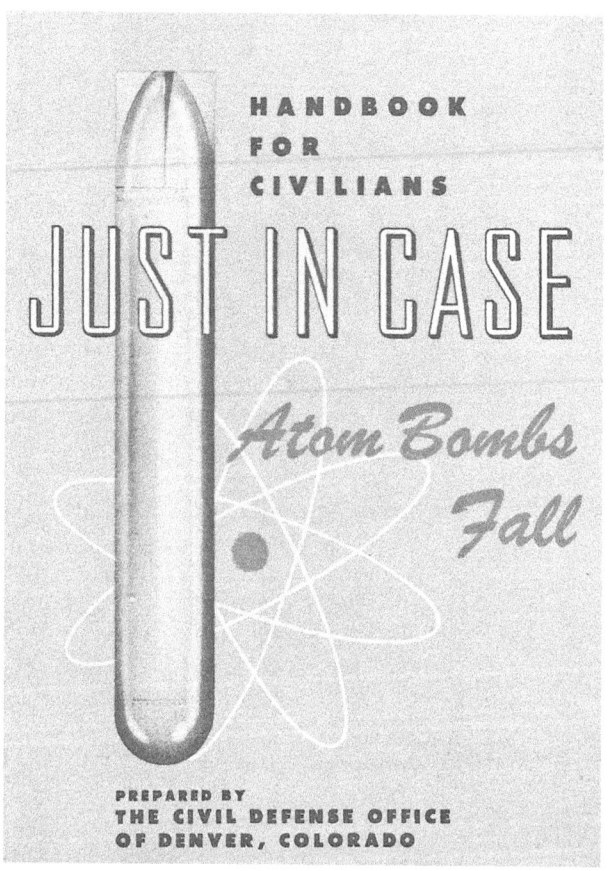

Just in Case Atom Bombs Fall, Civil Defense Office of Denver, 1951.

What to Do Before the Attack

1. KNOW YOUR OWN HOME, or the apartment house or hotel where you live. Know how to get to those parts of your residence that will probably afford you the greatest protection from a bombing. Generally speaking, well-constructed basements afford this protection (but be sure two exits exist, so that you can still get out if one is blocked). You are usually safer against a wall away from the center of the building, because there is less danger here from falling beams. Know where you keep your first-hand materials, fire-extinguishing devices, and extra quantities of food. Have flashlights ready.

2. STRIVE FOR FIRE-PROOF HOUSEKEEPING. Don't let trash pile up. Keep waste paper in covered containers. Store paints and other inflammable liq-

uids carefully. All parts of your house should be readily accessible, particularly the attic. Remove furniture, boxes, magazines, rags, and other inflammable materials from the attic. Distribute buckets of water or sand through your house if bombing attacks appear imminent. A shovel, heavy gloves, and a garden hose adapted to inside faucets would all come in handy for controlling fires.

IF YOU ARE AT HOME, and you hear the warning of an impending air attack, STAY AT HOME.

1. SHUT DOORS AND WINDOWS and pull down shades; this will help keep out fire sparks and radioactive dust. Shutters or venetian blinds, or heavy drapes, help protect you from flying glass.

2. WHEN AN ALERT SOUNDS, turn off your gas range burners and all other hand-operated gas appliances. Do all you can to eliminate sparks by shutting off the furnace. DO NOT turn off gas at the meter. DO NOT turn off your pilot lights. Turn off non-automatic gas appliances, such as manually-operated water heaters or room heaters. If your premises are NOT damaged by the attack, DO NOT USE GAS except for emergency purposes. If your premises ARE damaged, turn off gas at the meter if you can do so safely. IMPORTANT: once the gas valve at the meter is turned off, do not turn it on again yourself— call for a trained man. If you smell gas, extinguish all open flames. Do

The government constantly reminded Americans that an atomic blast could occur at any time on any day, and they must be ready—whether at home, at school, or on the street—to shield themselves immediately from the blinding flash.

not strike matches. Open doors and windows and get outside the buildings. Close fuel and draft doors on coal furnaces.

3. KEEP FLASHLIGHT HANDY. Don't strike matches because of the danger of blasts from leaking gas mains.

4. SHUT OFF VENTILATING FANS unless they are equipped with special filters to keep out radioactive dusts *[sic]*.

5. KEEP PETS INDOORS. Pets can bring in radioactive dust.

6. REMOVE YOUR CAR from the streets if you have ample warning. Leave streets open for emergency travel. Roll up car windows to keep out radioactive dust. DO NOT JUMP IN YOUR CAR in an effort to leave the city. You would be caught in slow-moving traffic. YOU WILL BE MUCH SAFER AT HOME.

7. BE CAREFUL OF WATER. A little water left standing in the pipes at the time of blast can be used. Wait for instructions on further use of water. Boiling water will not remove radioactivity, but will kill germs that might have gotten in through breaks in the mains.

8. DON'T TAKE CHANCES WITH FOOD in open containers. To prevent radioactive poisoning or disease, select your food with care. Stick to canned and bottled foods if possible.

9. IF NEAR THE BOMBED AREA, throw out unpackaged foods lying where dust might have settled on them. Wash outside of cans or bottles thoroughly before opening. Be sure utensils and tableware are clean. Food and utensils in closed drawers or tight cupboards will be safe to use.

10. SCRUB ALL CONTAMINATED OBJECTS in buckets or tubs used for that purpose only.

11. KEEP ALL WINDOWS AND DOORS CLOSED for at least several hours after an atomic bombing. Leave them shut until civil defense authorities determine there is no lingering radioactivity in your neighborhood. If there is serious contamination in your area, cover broken windows with blankets or cardboard.

12. CHILDREN AT SCHOOL SHOULD STAY AT SCHOOL. The schools are developing plans to provide maximum protection for children.

13. STAY AT HOME. Do not leave until civil defense authorities can determine what areas of the city would constitute no danger to you.

14. USE THE TELEPHONE ONLY FOR TRUE EMERGENCIES. Do not use the phone unless absolutely necessary. Leave the lines open for real emergency traffic.

During a Bombing Attack

1. KEEP COOL. Avoid chaos; prevent disorder and havoc.

2. STAY HOME. That is the safest place. If you are away from home, get under cover in the nearest shelter; avoid crowded places; stay off the streets; the enemy wants you to run out into the streets and create a panic.

3. LIE DOWN. This is the most important single thing you can do. Try to find protection. In buildings, keep away from the center of the floor, where danger of falling beams is much greater. You are also safer near a structural column of a building. Outside, keep away from trees or flimsy structures. Curl up to protect face, neck, and arms from flash burns.

4. AFTER EXPLOSION, keep away from radioactive dust. Keep home closed. Changes clothes. Take a shower. Remember, water safe for bathing purposes may not be safe for drinking, however. If caught outside, moisten handkerchief and use as a filter against breathing radioactive dust.

If You Have Only a Second's Warning

1. FALL FLAT ON YOUR FACE. This greatly lessens chances of blast injury; also of flash burns. More than half of all wounds result from being tossed about or from being struck by falling and flying objects.

2. IF YOU'RE IN A BUILDING. Flatten out close against the cellar wall; or any inside wall; or under a bed or table. Don't pick spot opposite windows because of flying glass.

3. IF OUTDOORS. Fall face-down against the base of a good substantial building; or a handy ditch or gutter. Don't look up; hold face in arms 10 or 12 seconds after blast to prevent burns and temporary blindness.

4. TO PREVENT FLASH BURNS. Try to find shelter, such as a high wall, high bank, or some solid object; if further away, even light cotton cloth will help.

Facts About the H Bomb

After the Soviet Union exploded a hydrogen bomb in August 1953—less than a year after the United States' first detonation of an H-bomb—a nuclear war became an even more frightening potentiality. The Federal Civil Defense Administration's 1955 brochure, Facts About the H Bomb, *outlined the new realities.*

When millions of Americans saw pictures of the tremendous fireball of the first hydrogen test explosion in "Operation Ivy," measuring 3¼ miles in diameter, many wondered how people in any large city could survive such a holocaust.

Yet the H-bomb, despite the wider range of its destructive force, will not destroy the earth.

There will always be much more of America undamaged, and many more millions of our people alive and eager to fight back and win, than there will be death and destruction.

Here are some of the facts we must learn to live with in what President Eisenhower has called "an age of peril."

1. Atomic bombs and hydrogen bombs do exist as deliverable weapons of war. The Russians are known beyond any doubt to possess a growing stockpile of such weapons.

2. Even the small atomic weapons now make one plane able to deliver as much destruction as could be carried by about 1,000 airplanes using conventional bombs in World War II.

3. No absolute military defense exists today or is likely to exist in the foreseeable future. A determined aggressor could deliver atomic or hydrogen bombs on our cities, should he decide to attack our country.

4. A bomb 1,000 times as powerful as the Hiroshima bomb will not cause damage 1,000 times as far away—*only 10 times as far*. It will harm an area only 100 times as large—not 1,000 times as large.

5. There are practical limits to the amount of destruction that can be caused by a single bomb of any kind.

6. The best means of protection from the immediate effects of atomic or hydrogen bombs are distance from the center of the explosion and the protection of suitable shelter.

7. Cooperate fully with your local civil defense authorities. They want to help you learn how to survive, if we are attacked. What you do *before* the explosion can save your life. What you do *after* the explosion can also save lives, including your own.

106   Part 4—Be Prepared

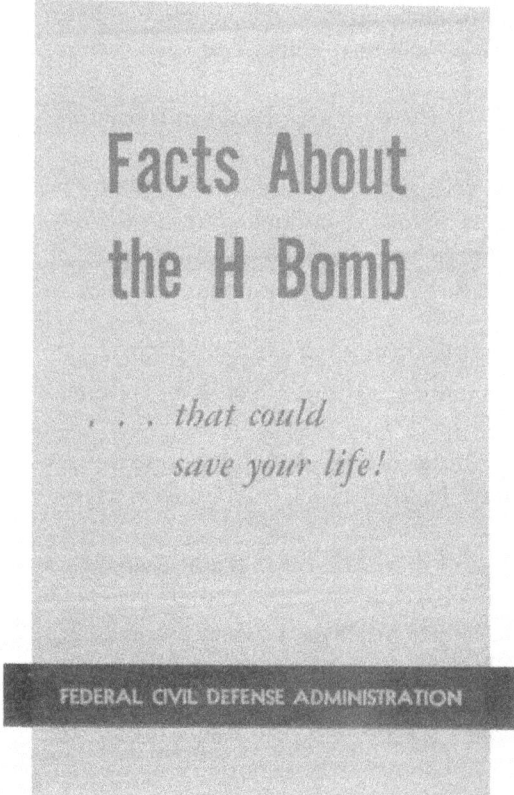

Facts About the H Bomb, Federal Civil Defense Administration, 1955.

What Are the Effects of Atomic or Hydrogen Bombs?

No matter how big the *size* of atomic weapons, we must concern ourselves with their *effects* on people and things. While the dividing lines between various damage areas of atomic blast are never sharp and clear cut, the effects are felt generally in four different areas.

1. The A-ring—a central area around the bull's-eye or Ground Zero in which destruction is so complete that neither people nor buildings have much chance of surviving.

2. The B-ring—a larger belt of heavy damage around the central area. This ring is about three times as large as the A-ring. In the B-ring, injury to people and destruction of buildings would be severe but not complete.

3. The C-ring—a still larger circular belt of lesser damage around the B-ring. Injuries to people in this area would range from moderate to light.

4. The D-ring—where damage would be light and all of the rest of the countryside beyond the limits of even light damage from the blast. However, much of this area can be affected by the fallout of radioactive particles resulting from certain kinds of nuclear attack.

If you live or work near the heart of a probable aiming point, it will take a well-rehearsed civil defense dispersal plan and early attack warning from the Air Force to evacuate you to safety when the alert sounds.

If you live or work within reach of secondary blast effects, in an area where damage probably would be heavy, dispersal is still your best chance of staying alive.

If you live so far from the center of a target area that damage probably would be light, you still need a home shelter for greater security from both blast and radioactive fall-out. And you should know how to render first aid, put out small fires, and take other civil defense measures to help yourself and others.

If you live well beyond any likely target area, you still need to know first aid, how to feed the hungry, shelter the homeless, and aid others less fortunate than yourself. And you should plan adequate cover against radioactive fall-out.

No longer can any American avoid the responsibility for learning everything possible about personal and community survival. All 160 million Americans at home must accept an active part in civil defense preparedness. Organized civil defense is both a shield and a sword. It can reduce appreciably the loss of lives and property under enemy attack, help us get back on our feet faster, maintain our will to win. But a sound civil defense, coupled with a strong military defense, can also help deter an enemy from starting a war by making aggression unprofitable.

The H-bomb is bigger than the A-bomb — but it is still a bomb. It has its limits, as does any other weapon. It makes the civil defense problem larger, but not different. Your survival actions are even more important — because they are actions that only you can take for the protection of yourself and your family.

Learn and practice civil defense preparedness in your home, your neighborhood, your community. Then, no matter what happens, you and your family — and the Nation — will be ready.

Don't Panic

Above all else, don't panic! That message wove its way into government pamphlets wherever possible. Your Civil Defense Manual: A Handbook on Personal Survival, *published by the Milwaukee Civil Defense Administration, not only described the Home Defense Corps, but also stressed that "panic can kill you."*

The physical damage effects of the Superbomb — blast, heat, and radiation — are believed by some to be less devastating than the psychological effects. "Subjective dangers" or mental hazards are what cause people trapped in burning hotels to jump out of the window to certain death, instead of waiting for the rescue that is on the way; to trample each other to death to get out of a burning movie theatre; or to run into the path of a tornado instead of seeking the shelter that would have saved them. Under severe provocation, anyone and everyone is subject to panic.

What Causes PANIC?

To understand what causes panic is to win half the battle against it. Psychologists are agreed that the principal causes are:

Danger — or threat of danger — with no apparent means of escape.
Inability to evaluate the true situation when the familiar every-day world falls to pieces.
Anxiety or fear, which has lain dormant in either the conscious or subconscious, and which is triggered to release by the emergency.

When the A-Bomb fell on Hiroshima and Nagasaki, the Japanese found that these three elements were the most perilous of all the effects of the bomb. Translated, then, into terms of that situation, causes of panic were:

The spectacle of the bomb and its after-effects.
The sight of casualties in overwhelming numbers and the havoc caused by the bomb.
Fear of another bomb.

Antidotes for PANIC

Having once understood what causes panic, and accepted the fact that anyone, given sufficient provocation, could panic, there are certain practical measures you may take which will make you virtually immune.

According to the government, preventing widespread panic represented one of the most critical issues during the 1950s. Americans needed to maintain self-control during an atomic attack. Otherwise, they might "be trapped in the blind alley of desperate, mindless, unreasoning panic" (*Your Civil Defense Manual: A Handbook on Personal Survival*, Milwaukee Civil Defense Administration, no date).

Danger—What to do?

Learn what to do when disaster strikes. More important still — practice it. Drill on it until your reaction is automatic — until it becomes second nature to you. That is the only substitute for previous experience, that is for having been through ten or a dozen previous bomb attacks. The person who knows what he should have done, but forgets it until the emergency is past, may never have a chance to remember.

Orientation

Get the facts. Believe nothing you cannot check. Turn your radio to Conelrad — follow the instructions of your Civil Defense organization and follow your Civil Defense plan. Doing these things will bring you out of it if your senses are temporarily frozen. Remember — panic is contagious and you must react to an emergency in an adult manner, not by childish imitation of those who cry havoc.

Anxiety

Disaster studies prove that a feeling of group security is a potent factor in reducing anxiety and thereby the chance that you will panic in an emergency. By volunteering for your local Civil Defense effort NOW, you will learn to work with the group who will take over if a bomb falls. You will have a definite place in the plan and a definite part in reducing the destruction and casualties. As soon as the warning sirens sound, your course will be charted and your duties and responsibilities will carry you through the first wave of hysteria which will inevitably follow the blast.

When you have accomplished these things, you will have achieved the emotional maturity necessary to survive and to help others to survive. Learn to be responsible for yourself and for others — responsibility is one of the strongest deterrents to blind, unreasoning hysteria. Learn to respect the rights and needs of others. The doctrine of "dog eat dog" benefits nobody but our enemies.

MOST IMPORTANT — You can set an example of self-control that will help to check the spread of terror and will save many lives — maybe your own — that would otherwise be trapped in the blind alley of desperate, mindless, unreasoning P A N I C !

3 Minutes of Your Time

As part of the country's overall civil defense effort, the government urged Americans to give blood as a demonstration of their commitment to democracy. 3 Minutes of Your Time Can Save a Life, *published in 1953, explained the need for blood for national emergencies, including an atomic attack.*

Recognizing blood as a critical national resource vital to the country's well-being and security, [President Eisenhower] directed the establishment of the National Blood Program to provide for the total blood needs of the Nation. In accordance with this directive, the American National Red Cross, the Department of Defense, and the Federal Civil Defense Administration joined efforts and pooled resources to make the National Blood Program a success.

However, in our American Democracy, the Government's efforts depend on the cooperation of the Nation's 150 million citizens. It is you, the reader, who must heed the President's urgent plea for blood. Without your cooperation, the Government is powerless to build the needed supply of this critical resource....

Over Main Street, YOUR hometown, enemy bombers, lost in the high noon sun, drone out a frightful noon Angelus. Atomic thunder evokes all to prayer. Great blasts of wind and searing heat rush outward from the explosion, leaving a wake of destruction. A deathly silence settles over the debris, pierced only by the occasional cry of the wounded and dying, and the sobs of the bereaved. YOUR town is dying.

On this day, if it comes, how far will your family and friends be from the havoc circling ground zero? How much blood will they need to recover from their wounds? Will they die with the town for lack of blood?

Along the battlefront or in your very home, the need for blood might come at any moment.

3 Minutes of Your Time Can Save a Life, Federal Civil Defense Administration, 1953.

The American National Red Cross, U.S. Department of Defense, and the Federal Civil Defense Administration teamed up to encourage Americans to donate blood for any catastrophe, including an atomic attack, in which the need for blood would be "beyond comprehension."

In the event of atomic attack, the need for blood will be beyond comprehension. When fires raze and floods envelop, when disease strikes, human blood helps wage the battle of life. Gamma globulin, a blood derivative, is now being used to fight measles, hepatitis, and the crippling effects of polio. There must be an available reserve of this life-giving resource that will sustain our Nation in any emergency.

Common Sense

What to do, where to go, whom to contact—Americans heard this again and again. Be Prepared, *published in 1955 by the Denver Civil Defense Program, asked the question, "Where were you at 9:30 this morning?"*

Imagine, for a moment, that a foreign enemy dropped an atomic bomb on Denver at 9:30 a.m. today.

WHERE WERE YOU? Were you one of the unfortunate thousands that were close to the bomb blast?

WERE YOU KILLED?

WERE YOU PAINFULLY BURNED?

WERE YOU CRUSHED IN THE DEBRIS OF THE BOMB BLAST?

WHAT HAPPENED TO YOUR WIFE—where was she when the bomb burst? Is she alive? Is she injured? How can you find out whether she is still living? If she is injured, where can you find her? How can you learn the extent of her injuries? Is she frantically trying to find you to learn whether you are safe?

WERE YOUR CHILDREN AT SCHOOL? Were they injured? Where are they now?

DO YOUR CHILDREN HAVE A HOME LEFT TO GO TO?

IF YOU, YOUR WIFE, OR YOUR CHILDREN WERE INJURED, WHAT IS BEING DONE TO HELP YOU? Who is going to dig the debris away to rescue you? Where does the blood plasma come from that can save your life? Who will try to strengthen the thread of life with emergency first aid? Who will rush a doctor to your side?

These are questions that only YOU, as a citizen of Denver, can answer. YOU can answer these questions in only one way—**BY SUPPORTING THE DENVER CIVIL DEFENSE PROGRAM.**

Denver would be a critical target in the event of an aerial attack on the United States. Long-range bombers exist today capable of carrying out such an attack. Our best defenses could not prevent some of them from getting through.

For a year and a half, Denver city officials have built the foundation and organization of a civil defense program.

Local facilities have been built up for the protection of life and property—facilities in both equipment and manpower. This will be periodically reviewed so that it may be kept currently effective.

Be Prepared, Denver Civil Defense Program, 1955.

That was the first phase of the plan.

The second phase of the plan — training the people of Denver to meet with composure, with intelligence, with knowledge, a war-borne catastrophe — is about to begin.

Denver is mobilizing for the protection of its people, its homes, its businesses, its industry.

YOU will make this second phase work. This second phase is the "ace in the hole." It is Denver's reserve strength and power, to be prepared and held ready to release if and when needed.

No one has the right to expect protection or the benefits and blessings of freedom unless he is willing to assume the obligations of citizenship.

That means positive action. That means immediate steps to cope with the possibility of a sudden attack by a powerful aggressor armed with the most devastating weapons modern warfare can produce.

Support of the Denver Civil Defense effort means more, to you, than a patriotic duty. It is **SELF-PRESERVATION**.

YOU and your neighbors must learn that there is a right and wrong answer for emergency situations. Then you must learn that right answer.

EVERY JOB IN CIVIL DEFENSE MUST BE MANNED CAPABLY AND DEVOTEDLY.

By enrolling in the Denver Civil Defense program, you will be taught how to protect yourself, your family, your neighbors, and your city.

You'll learn the specific ways to save life and property, including your own. You will take part in the **TRAINING PROGRAM FOR SURVIVAL**.

The safety of you and your family may rest with the service of a well-trained neighbor. His safety may depend on **YOU**.

The Denver Civil Defense program needs thousands of people training in first aid — the first aspect of the training program. It needs people trained in special skills: nurses aides, food handlers, welfare workers, the clergy.

CIVIL DEFENSE BEGINS WITH YOU — WITH YOUR ENROLLMENT AND TRAINING.

YOUR ACTION MIGHT SAVE YOUR OWN LIFE AND THAT OF YOUR FAMILY.

Preparedness costs only your time and your effort.

BE PREPARED!

*Part 5*

Duck and Cover

Civil Defense for Schools, Pennsylvania State Council of Civil Defense, 1952.

"Atomics" in Education

In 1946, Aaron Goff, a junior high school teacher in Newark, New Jersey, coined the term "atomics" to refer to the incorporation of atomic topics and themes into the school curriculum — from kindergarten through senior high school. "Atomics" is in evidence in Civil Defense for Schools, *published in 1952 by the Pennsylvania State Council of Civil Defense. Although specifically for Pennsylvania teachers, the publication's recommendations reflect similar suggestions implemented by school districts across the country.*

A. General Suggestions for Teachers

1. Familiarize yourself with all available literature on how to survive an atomic bomb. Adapt this information to the particular group of pupils with whom you are working. If there are questions for which you lack answers, contact your local civil defense officials.

2. Sometimes children are troubled or worried by stories about war or bombings. They hear of such possibilities in the conversations of adults or over the radio. They see war pictures in booklets, at the movies, or on television. If they voice fears or ask questions, encourage them to talk. By so doing, you can help the children in two ways. First, merely expressing fears helps reduce "tensions." Second, you can give them correct information on how to protect themselves from an atomic bomb and increase their confidence in their ability to survive an attack.

3. A possible method of introducing the subject of atomic bombs and instructions concerning the safety procedures is outlined in the following sections. As much time as is needed should be given to this instruction. Too much should not be given at any one time. At the end of each day's lesson, you should review with the children the information they will talk over that night with their parents.

4. When you give your pupils information about the bomb, ask them to take copies home. The material may be duplicated (mimeographed, hectographed, multigraphed, etc.) by the school; or, older children may take notes and write it down under the direction of the teacher.

5. Encourage students to discuss the material taken home with their parents, and keep it for later reference. Also encourage the children and their parents to bring to the school any questions they may have after home discussion of the information.

6. From time to time, review essential information with the pupils. Just after an air raid drill may be a favorable time to reemphasize key safety procedures.

Civil Defense for Schools, Pennsylvania State Council of Civil Defense, 1952.

7. While this material stresses protection from atomic bombs, shelter is the basic form of protection from all kinds of attack. Just remember that it sometimes may be necessary to leave the building shortly after a raid, particularly if fire, or incendiary, bombs are dropped.

8. Explain to children that their parents will know these rules and follow the same ones wherever they may be. In this way, you may relieve children's anxieties about their parents.

9. In teaching the essential facts and procedures necessary for self-protection, it is most important to teach the children WITHOUT FRIGHTENING THEM.

10. Subject matter for all grades should include:
    a. Taking cover — how, where, and why.
    b. Conduct on way to and from school, on the playground, and over weekends.
    c. Conduct when separated from the family.
       (1) Younger children should know the full name, address, and telephone number of parents.
       (2) Younger children should be familiar with appearance of policemen and civil defense workers and taught how to seek them out in emergencies.
       (3) Older children should be well versed in general preparedness, including preparation of first aid kits, use of fire fighting equipment, and procurement of emergency food and water supplies.

11. Older children, in addition, can be taught:
    a. What they can do at home to help develop home preparedness:
       (1) Helping their mothers equip the home, first aid kits, emergency food shelf, fire extinguishers, flashlights, lanterns, etc.
       (2) Helping mothers close the house if the alarm sounds.
    b. Living like pioneers:
       (1) Prepare children for the possibility of being without a stove, water, electricity, gas — like camping out.
       (2) Tie this aspect in with scouting. Thus, without scaring them, you prepare them for the possibility of widespread devastation. If they are prepared to "live like pioneers," they will be a help, rather than a hindrance, in time of crisis. Appeal to such groups as Boy Scouts, Girl Scouts, Junior Red Cross organizations, etc.

B. Suggestions for Teachers and Pupils

1. *If the Warning Signal Sounds*
   a. When children are in school:
      (1) Go to the shelter quickly and quietly.
      (2) Pupils should be instructed that, in case any of them are out of the room when the warning sounds, they should go to the shelter by the most direct route and report at once to the teacher.
   b. When the children are on the playground:
      (1) Listen for the whistle of the teacher.

    (2) Go directly to the teacher for instructions.
  c. When children are walking or bicycling to or from the school:
    (1) If the child is on foot, he should run to the nearest house or shelter.
    (2) If near the school, he should be instructed to return to the school.
    (3) If near his home, he should return home at once.
    (4) If more than 5 or 6 minutes from either home or school, he should seek shelter in a nearby house or building.
    (5) If he is not near a building, he should lie down at once as he has been instructed to do at school, either in the gutter, near a curb, or behind any form of shelter.
  d. If children are in a bus, they should obey the instructions of the bus driver. (It is important that bus drivers be given complete instructions by school authorities.)
  e. If the children are in a private conveyance, the driver will stop the vehicle at once and occupants will proceed to the nearest shelter. (This might well be a subject of a letter to parents, asking their cooperation on this point.)
2. *If There Is No Warning, but a Very Bright Light in the Sky*
  a. When children are in school they should:
    (1) Lie face down on the floor under a desk or table and bury their faces in their arms.
    (2) Remain there until instructed to get up or move.
  b. If out-of-doors, the children should:
    (1) Quickly lie face down and bury faces in their folded arms.
    (2) Remain there at least until the "debris stops falling," or until instructed to move by a "grown-up."
3. *When the "All-Clear" Signal Sounds*
  a. If in school, the pupils should either go back to their classrooms, or assemble outside the buildings, as directed by their teachers.
  b. If en route to or from school, children should be taught to follow the instructions of the bus driver or some other "grown-up" nearby. (Older children should be instructed to watch what older people do and then, if it appears to be in order, to proceed on their way.)

C. Suggestions for Kindergarten to Grade Three

1. *Talking It Over with Children*
  a. Comparatively few teaching materials have been developed for children in these grades. The necessary information should be presented as gradually and as naturally as possible. This can be done best by talking it over with the children and answering their questions.
  b. The information presented in this booklet is up-to-date and accurate and should be used by all teachers. The method and language used will vary according to the maturity of the children. Probably several days should be taken to present the information. Third grade children may require fewer

lessons and less repetition than younger children. The teacher's most important responsibility is to be calm and assuring and to allay the fears of the children.

2. *Possible Conversational Approaches Which a Teacher May Use*
    a. "How many of you have ever seen Norman Harris' program, LIVING WONDERS, or the ZOO PARADE on television? What have you learned about the ways in which plants and animals protect themselves?"
    b. "How have the people in our country had to protect themselves in days gone by from Indian attacks, storms, floods, etc.?"
    c. "What dangers do we face every day from automobiles, fires, and on the playground?"
    d. "What are some of the things we have learned already about taking care of ourselves?" Likely answers include:
       (1) "We walk through a building and we do not run."
       (2) "We stop at the red light when we are walking to school."
       (3) "We watch for the policeman's signal before crossing streets."
       (4) "In a fire drill, we walk quickly and quietly out of the building."
       (To list given answers on the blackboard, or a special chart, may prove helpful.)
    e. "How many of you like to see cowboy movies, or watch Hopalong Cassidy and the Lone Ranger on television?"
    f. "Have any of you seen pictures, in the paper or on television, of soldiers fighting in Korea?"
    g. "How is the fighting in Korea different from the kind you see in cowboy pictures?
       (1) In the discussion which follows, the kinds of weapons will probably be discussed. This should lead to some mention of the atomic bomb.
       (2) After finding out how much children already know, or think they know about it, the teacher can then go on with the material included under *Some Things Children Need to Know*.
       (It may be that little discussion or understanding of questions *f* and *g* is either possible, or desirable, with kindergarten children. Perhaps the most we should expect of them is that they understand the necessary safety rules and follow them.)

3. *Some Things Children Need to Know*
    a. "On the 4th of July, you have seen or heard firecrackers or fireworks. They make a loud noise and a bright flash. If you are not too close, they do you no harm. Of course, if you are even a little careless, you can be hurt by firecrackers. That is why, in many states, we have laws against the sale of them."
    b. "A bomb is something like a big firecracker. It makes a loud noise and a very bright flash. We hope that a bomb may never fall on our town or any part of our country. But let's find out enough about the atomic bomb to learn to take care of ourselves should it strike."
    c. "First of all, if any enemy airplanes were coming, we would probably receive

a warning in time to get to a safe place. A safe place is a shelter. A house, a garage, a schoolhouse, a store, a subway, or a library can be a shelter. Let us find out how to get to the shelter in our schoolhouse."
- (1) It is important to present the idea of the shelter gradually, in order not to arouse unnecessary fear.
- (2) Plan to have familiar materials in the school shelter.
- (3) Take children to shelter occasionally for songs, story telling, or for dramatization. Let them get used to the idea of going to the shelter.

d. "We have never had a bad fire in any of our schools, but you know that we have fire drills often, so that we can learn how to take care of ourselves if there were a fire. In just the same way we are going to have some new drills, which we will call air raid drills. We don't expect to need these drills, but again we want to know how to take care of ourselves. This time our drills are going to take us to special places inside our building (or, for some schools, inside a nearby building). Let us plan how to go quickly and quietly to our shelter."
- (1) Make a chart of the children's responses to the suggestion of a plan. Be sure ALL of the following facts are stated and are understood by the children:
  - (a) "When we hear the signal, we must STOP, LOOK at the teacher, and LISTEN."
  - (b) "We must GO TO THE SHELTER at once."
  - (c) "We must GO QUIETLY."
  - (d) "We must NOT PUSH against each other as we walk in line."

e. "Now let's go down to our shelter and play some games there."
- (1) After returning to the classroom, the teacher should be sure that the children understand the lesson on preparedness.
- (2) The next day the teacher should review the previous day's lesson, drawing from children the information they learned.
- (3) Teachers may find it desirable to make a chart, appropriate to the grade level, of this information.

D. Suggestions for Grades Four to Seven

1. *Talking It Over with the Pupils*
   a. What are some of the ways by which plants and animals protect themselves?
   b. How have the people in our country had to protect themselves?
      - (1) In colonial and frontier days?
      - (2) During past wars?
      - (3) From the forces of nature?
      - (4) From hazards of sports, transportation, etc.?
   c. What are some of the ways we have already learned to protect ourselves today?
      - (1) In school?
      - (2) At home?

(3) On the street?
(4) In public places?
d. Have children ever had to protect themselves against bombs?
  (1) In England, school children learned safety rules and went to shelter areas when necessary.
  (2) They continued with their education, and only a few out of the many thousands in schools were hurt.
e. Why does the present state of emergency make it urgent that we learn new ways of protecting ourselves?
f. What do you know about the atomic bomb?
g. How many of you have read about the bomb experiments at Bikini? In Nevada?
  (1) There were 42,000 men at the two atomic explosions which government scientists set off at Bikini.
  (2) Not a single one of those 42,000 men was hurt by atomic rays, although two bombs were exploded and there was plenty of danger.
h. Let us see some of the things we need to know about atomic bombs, and how to protect ourselves against injuries possibly caused by them.

2. *Things the Pupils Should Know*
  a. If you have been reading papers, listening to the radio, or watching television, you know that our country is facing many problems at this time. To make matters worse, some papers and news commentators make the news sound more serious than it is.
  b. The United States has faced many crises in its history and has always come through them successfully. The population of the United States is made up of a proud, courageous people. They are not people to shiver at the thought of danger. You boys and girls are the descendants of thousands of men and women who fought to stay alive.
  c. Today, many people are talking about atomic energy, about its benefits as well as its danger. Every day men and women are learning of new helpful uses of this power in medicine, industry, and agriculture.
  d. Many people are worrying about the atomic bomb, yet they have not tried to learn much about it. Too few of us know that many of the earlier reports of the bomb's supposedly mysterious powers are not true. The truth is not nearly so bad as most people think, for protection is possible.
  e. We are not trying to fool you about the bomb, but we do want to tell you how to protect yourselves at school and on the way to and from school. Should the bomb strike, these same rules will help you wherever you may be.

3. *How Afraid Should I Be of the Atomic Bomb?*
  a. We need not fear it very much. We are much more likely to have an accident at home or from an automobile than to be injured by an atomic bomb.
  b. We do need to know, however, what the bomb does and how to take care of ourselves. Ignorance makes fear. Fear makes panic. Panic might cause more trouble than a bomb.

4. *What Does the Bomb Do?*

a. The bomb has "KNOCKDOWN POWER." Its "blast wave" is like a powerful sudden wind that starts out from the exploding weapon at about ten times the speed of a hurricane, or 1,000 miles per hour.
   (1) A low hill or even a high earthen bank may completely cut off the blast.
   (2) If you have only a second's warning, there is one important thing you can do to lessen your chances of injury by blast—FALL FLAT, FACE DOWN, and bury your face in your arms.
b. The bomb gives off a flash of light and heat. Usually people speak of this action of the bomb by the one word, HEAT.
   (1) The HEAT FLASH comes at the moment the bomb goes off. It lasts several seconds. The flash makes a light so bright that people can see it several hundred miles away, even in the daytime. It will probably blind you a few seconds or minutes if your eyes are open and you are close to it—just as any strong light like a searchlight can blind you for a time.
   (2) The HEAT that comes with the flash can cause unprotected people and animals to get painfully burned. But this heat can easily be stopped. It lasts only about three seconds. Materials such as heavy cloth or stiff pasteboard will not let the heat flash pass through.
c. The bomb gives off atomic rays or radiation.
   (1) These rays are given off when the bomb explodes. You can't see them. You can't feel them. You may even be hit by them and go right on without even knowing it. Neither can you see nor feel X-rays when a doctor uses them for a treatment or to take an X-ray picture, but the rays are there. The sun and stars also give off radiation. Too long exposure to the sun's rays in the summer can burn you and make you ill. We call that "sunburn."
   (2) Although these rays are powerful and dangerous, if you are near the point where a bomb explodes, you can protect yourself from these rays. Some of the things that will protect you are:
      (a) Buildings.
      (b) Walls of buildings.
      (c) Air-raid shelters.
      (d) Earth around the cellar of a house.
      (e) An ordinary ditch.
d. Additional facts about the effects of the atomic bomb.
   (1) The rays will NOT, as some people think, kill you if you just get a little of them. It all depends on the amount you get.
   (2) The rays will NOT make it dangerous for someone else to touch you if you, yourself, have been touched by the rays. People CANNOT catch from other people the sickness which atomic rays may cause.
   (3) The use of the atomic bomb will NOT make the whole world unfit to live in.
      (a) It would take a huge number of the bombs—almost a million of them, all exploded at about the same time—to make the world unsafe for human life.

(b) One bomb is exceedingly expensive and no nation will ever have a million of them.
(c) The plant and animal records we have from the Japanese bombings and the Pacific Island test prove that animals made sick by bomb rays often recover completely.
(d) Plants have grown right back on the ground where atomic bombs were used.

E. Suggestions for Grades Eight to Twelve

1. *Introducing the Subject*
   a. People have always had to protect themselves from other peoples, forces of nature, the products of man's ingenuity and inventiveness, hazards of transportation, etc.
   b. Protective procedures and devices have been found to combat these dangers.
   c. The crisis in the United Nations, Korea, Red China, Russia, and the like warns us of danger.
   d. The present national emergency, the need for civil defense, the steps taken in your own town, are necessary protective measures.
   e. Man's recent release of atomic energy, first accomplished during World War II, combined with six years of increasing knowledge of its uses, indicates a need for protection.
   f. The beneficial and destructive possibilities of sudden releases of tremendous amounts of energy:
      (1) Mt. Etna.
      (2) Electricity.
      (3) Natural gas.
      (4) TNT.
      (5) Atomic energy.
   g. The challenge of atomic energy:
      (1) Another type of powerful explosive.
      (2) A means to improve living conditions.
      (3) Its development and control essential.
      (4) A deterrent to aggression.
      (5) Protection against its destructive forces.
2. *Things the Students Should Know*
   (See Suggestions For Grades Four To Seven on preceding pages. Improvise or elaborate on this material to suit the particular age level of students being taught.)
3. *How Much Should We Fear the Atomic Bomb?*
   a. Not as much as some people think. To be sure, it is powerful. Also, however, the bomb is less disastrous than we once were told it was. We are in more danger from lightning or from an automobile accident.
   b. The major damage (85%) from an atomic bomb is the same as from other

types of bombs. People protected themselves from these. We all know that in England during World War II, people continued to live, work, go to school, despite all the bombs dropped on the country.
   c. One of the worst dangers could be from panic; from people not knowing what to do; or from people rushing about blocking roads, bridges, and tunnels. Learning the rules for protection is essential to safety.
4. *What Are the Characteristics of an Atomic Bomb?*
   (See Suggestions for Grades Four to Seven, *What Does the Bomb Do?* Present this subject matter on a more mature level, suited to the particular age group, or level, of the students.)

Atomic Activities

The Georgia Office of Civil Defense, in Civil Defense Manual for Georgia Schools *(1952), expanded on "atomics" by outlining how schools could incorporate atomic topics in the curriculum, as well as high school organizations and extracurricular activities, such as writing articles for the school newspaper and making posters for bulletin boards.*

Suggestions for High School Groups

STUDENT COUNCIL ...
Chapel programs, to get everybody defense-minded, may well be handled by this organization.

Sponsoring of an Honor Roll, to post names of rooms that have put up defense poster on wall, or students who have posted defense instructions on wall at home, will lend prestige and dignity to student achievement toward defense.

SCHOOL PAPER ...
Editor and staff can be particularly helpful in writing and publishing articles about the defense program in general, and special achievements of grades or individual students.

LIBRARY ...
The librarian and her staff can be invaluable in displaying interesting and informative books, pamphlets, magazine articles, etc., for faculty and students. Many librarians call attention at chapel or faculty meetings to special articles appearing in the latest magazines about the defense program.

ART DEPARTMENT ...
There is nothing more powerful than eye-taking posters and bulletin boards to arouse interest in the defense program. Recognition in chapel for the best defense posters, for the most appealing bulletin board, for illustrations of stick figures and other drawing that may be used in letters to parents and other defense publications of the school, will encourage art-minded, talented students to contribute much of great value to defense efforts.

SCIENCE CLASSES ...
Study of atomic warfare, chemical warfare, and biologic warfare will give students an insight into the present dangerous situations. Boys in the vocational agriculture classes will be especially interested in biologic warfare, which constitutes a special threat to Georgia agriculture. Stress many things already being done (getting rid of rats and other vermin, sanitary disposal of garbage, reporting of any crop failures or animal diseases, learning about gases, poisons, etc.) that will stand community in good stead in emergency.

Civil Defense Manual for Georgia Schools, Georgia Office of Civil Defense, 1952.

Top: Whether in class or school corridors, students were never far from images of the atomic bomb, such as "eye-taking posters and bulletin boards to arouse interest in the defense program." *Bottom:* Science classes gave students a hands-on opportunity to experiment with atomic energy, including the principles of atomic bombs.

PHYSICAL EDUCATION ...

It is possible that the physical education instructor may be in charge of the defense drills, and organizing the schools to get students and teachers into safety shelters. Older boys and girls should be given much of responsibility for this.

Recreation: Britain found that it is vital for youngsters to have morale preserved during times of danger. Training older boys and girls to help with simple games, stories, songs, etc., for smaller children is a good idea.

Mental health will be a big part of this general health program under this area. Every student and teacher should be aware of these general things:

> Don't start rumors — don't believe wild stories.
> Radiation sickness does not always cause death.
> Most diseases spread slowly.
> Germ warfare will not knock out entire cities.
> Poisons cannot kill millions, and no mystery germs can cause panic-rousing epidemics.
> People who have mild exposures to nerve gases will usually recover.

Technical bulletins easily available, and chapters in most modern texts, offer endless possibilities for fact replacing rumor and fear in the cultivation of both physical and mental fear for our people in daily life and in emergency.

HOMEMAKING CLASSES ...

Girls and boys in these classes can strengthen the defense program by doing a good job of many things already on their activity list: first aid, home health, nutrition, child care and development of harmonious family living, good cooking, growing and preserving foods, etc.

BUSINESS DEPARTMENTS ...

Schools will be used in most instances for hospitals in case of emergency. Forms will be sent for filling out so that health authorities can find out what space is available, floor plans, etc. The commercial students can be of help here. They could also take over the responsibility for making records of local resource people, who can drive cars, who has had first aid courses, who knows about fire fighting, which homes could accommodate refugees or have extra rooms or cots, etc.

These are by no means suggestions for all classes. Each will think up ways to help. No more revealing situation can be imagined to find out who is really emotionally mature and who is sensitive, easily hurt, uncooperative, than in the defense planning. The fine, mature teacher or student will quickly fall in line, find ways to be useful, and lend his unique talents and abilities to building a sound school program. These are also the ones you can count on in emergencies. They are good to have around!

Other schools — and your state office — would be genuinely appreciative for any new ideas you have or any ways you have found particularly good that will help others to do a good job of getting Georgia schools ready to take their full responsibilities in a crisis which all of us devoutly hope never arises.

But remember ...
PREPARATION PREVENTS PANIC. BE PREPARED!

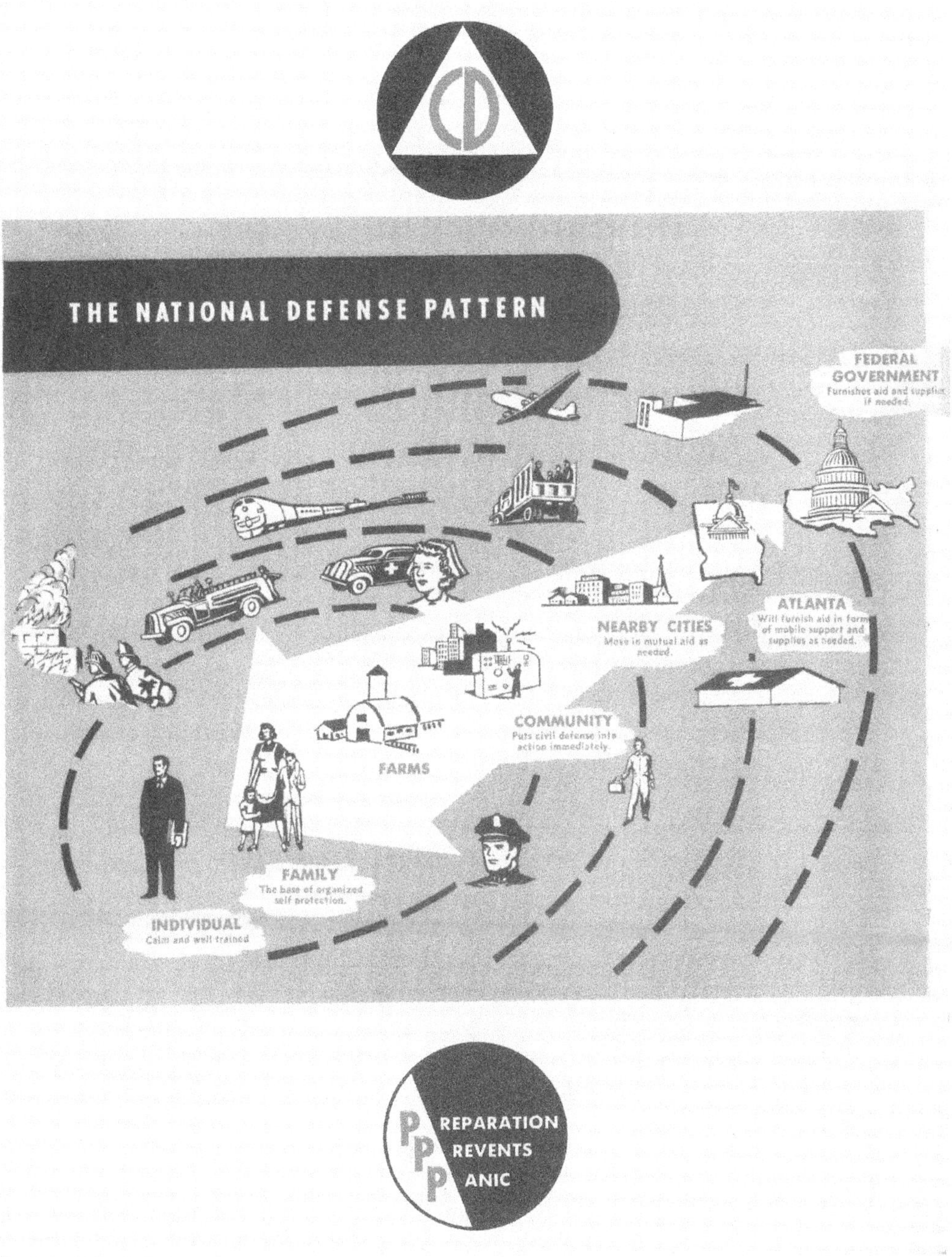

The National Defense Pattern began with the individual, who was calm and well trained. From there, it moved to the family, farms, communities, cities, and, at the top, the federal government. The motto, heard again and again: Preparation Prevents Panic (*Civil Defense Manual for Georgia Schools*, Georgia Office of Civil Defense, 1952).

Prepare for the Worst

With the massive destructive power of the hydrogen bomb, schools had to have contingency plans both for moving to shelters and for evacuating students to safe areas. In either event, schools had to take steps to reduce anxiety and lessen fear among students. Civil Defense in Oregon Schools, *published in 1958 by the Oregon State Civil Defense Agency, covered all these topics.*

As the power of nuclear weapons has increased, their destructive range has become so extended that shelter or refuge areas in existing structures may be of little value even at a distance of several miles from the center of an explosion. Such areas within a school building can provide only a limited form of protection. School authorities must, therefore, consider evacuation as well as shelter (refuge) plans, basing their decisions, as in all civil defense matters, upon local circumstances and needs. The desirability of evacuation as a survival measure depends on a number of factors, including the nature and severity of the danger under consideration. Even in some peacetime disasters, evacuation in necessary. In fire drills, for example, children are trained to leave both the building and its immediate vicinity. In the case of nuclear attack, Portland and Klamath Falls have no alternative, and evacuation is the only reasonably sure protection. The effectiveness of pre-disaster evacuation depends upon (a) the amount of warning time, (b) the availability of evacuation routes and adequate transportation facilities, and (c) the degree to which behavior is governed by previous training, including an understanding of the procedures and experience in practice drills.

Plans for schools in the Portland and Klamath Falls target areas should provide for evacuation of the school population directly to support areas, with plans worked out to cover such items as:

- Adequate and available transportation.
- Special training of drivers, including routes to be followed, their relation to general community evacuation routes, and alternate plans in case of road blocks or other obstructions.
- Loading plans, charting of routes for reaching the loading area on point.
- Emergency welfare center or school in an area outside the target area to which the children are to be delivered.
- Adequate reception and care facilities in support areas.
- Procedures for acquainting parents with the evacuation plans.

CIVIL DEFENSE IN OREGON SCHOOLS

. . . A PLANNING AND INSTRUCTION GUIDE

Civil Defense in Oregon Schools, Oregon State Civil Defense Agency, 1958.

- Trained leaders to take charge of groups while en route and upon arrival in an emergency welfare center or school outside the evacuation area.

Plans for schools in non-target areas should show that children are dispatched to their homes rather than evacuated to a support area; planning should include:

- A map of the community to show residence locations of the school population and whether or not a responsible adult is normally at home during school hours.

- Records of alternate arrangements for pupils when parents are temporarily not at home and for those whose parents are normally at work during the school day.
- Procedures for gathering in loading areas.
- Routes to be followed by pupil groups in going home and essential special provisions for those whose ordinary routes would cross general evacuation lines.
- Trained leaders to take charge of groups in emergency welfare centers.
- Trained escorts for young children who may need the help of a teacher or older pupil in getting home.

All dispersal plans assume a pre-disaster warning allowing adequate time for evacuation to the support areas. It is possible, however, that the time interval might not be long enough to accomplish this objective; unforeseeable developments might occasion delay or necessitate changes in procedure. It might still be advantageous to start the evacuation. The saving of lives begins as soon as people start moving out of congested areas. As distance from the center of disaster is increased, so are the chances of survival increased. Under such circumstances, each evacuating group will endeavor by all possible means to reach an emergency welfare center, but it must also be ready to identify the best available improvised shelter or refuge when further movement is no longer possible or advisable.

For a really adequate protection program, every school must make plans for shelter or refuge areas on the school grounds. These may, in locations removed from target centers, be sufficient protection for all likely emergencies, including danger from radioactive fallout. They are necessary, too, in case evacuation plans must be abandoned or in case disaster strikes with insufficient warning. The following steps indicate in a general way the planning that is needed:

- Survey the school building to identify shelter assets and hazards.
- Select and map out areas suitable for use as a shelter or refuge. If these areas will not accommodate the school population, make plans for needed additional facilities.
- Provide necessary supplies and equipment.
- Assign pupil groups and plan assembling procedures.

Both evacuation plans and shelter or refuge provisions are designed to care for children during school hours. A different type of problem is involved in protection during the hours when pupils are going to and from school. Drivers of school buses should be qualified to look after large groups of children, and each one should be thoroughly familiar with the possible emergency refuges or shelters on his regular route. Pupils who walk to school should be made clearly aware of their responsibility for their own safety—that in case of sudden danger they should seek the nearest available shelter. A community survey to identify suitable buildings or other forms of protection would provide the information which each child might use in locating the places on his home-school route that would serve as his personal protection landmarks.

Working out the plans for providing adequate physical protection through evacuation or shelters is essentially an administrative function involving coordination of the whole school unit. Equally important is the responsibility for instructing pupils in the procedures to be followed and for preparing them to meet the shock effects of disaster. In this task, the role of the teacher is all-important.

Training Lessens Anxiety

Experience in foreign countries and investigations in our own have shown that children do not develop anxiety under stress conditions if they have been properly prepared to deal with these problems and have confidence in themselves and their adult associates. This psychological feeling of security, while it can be developed only gradually over a long period of time, results from teaching that in itself demonstrates the qualities of calmness and confidence which it seeks to engender in children. How the teacher works with the class is as important as the actual understandings and skills that are developed. How the teacher works with the class also influences the attributes of parents with reference to the plans of the school and in relation to the community civil defense program.

Effective plans for the instruction of children in survival behavior should provide for attention to two essential areas:

1. Significant information about various types of disasters, such materials to be as accurate and complete as present available knowledge can make them; and
2. Specific behavior appropriate in various types of emergencies, including ways in which each individual can help himself and, in addition, be of assistance to others either independently or under adult guidance.

As in all instructions, methods and materials must be adapted to the maturity level of the learner. Each pupil should become familiar with (a) the overall plans for the school unit and (b) the specific ways in which he should behave in an emergency. In developing the latter aspect, cooperative planning at the class group level is possible and desirable even with very young children, so that they may understand better not only what they should do but why such behavior is needed and how they, as individuals, fit into the larger school plan. The scope of this instruction would include both shelter and evacuation procedures. It should also recognize that the school day and year represent only a very small part of a child's total time, when compared with after-school hours, weekends, holidays, and vacations.

Emergencies may well occur at times when children are not in school, and instruction should give attention to appropriate behavior when on the street, at home, downtown, using public transportation, or in the park. Community civil defense plans should be explained and the relationship of the school's program to the overall plan made clear. Students and parents may thus be helped to understand why there is no single, uniform plan for all schools and how the varied procedures of different schools are coordinated in the larger whole.

In addition to learning the routines to be followed, children should become familiar with many activities appropriate to a "waiting" time. Every possible preparation should be made to avoid idleness. The skilled teacher, in planning for this part of the program, will organize it to realize educational values as well as prevent restlessness and anxiety among the pupils. Young children will need suggestions and guidance from an older person in keeping busy with such things as small toys, puzzle pictures, finger plays, and picture books. Listening to stories read or told can be alternated with activities allowing for relaxing movement within a restricted area. Elementary children can take care of themselves quite effectively if they have interest and activities to pursue. Teachers at this level can provide such resources as manipulative puzzles, table games, books, guessing games, and games permitting limited gross physical movement. Both individual and small group activities should be included for this age group.

Older students will need little attention if plans have been made with them to pursue appropriate individual or small group interests. Those of high-school age especially may prefer an active part in the civil defense program. They can learn to perform certain types of operations and thus free the adults for more difficult and specialized tasks. For example, they can serve as messengers and can assume clerical and registration functions. By learning the stories and games suitable for younger children, they can become effective assistants to or perhaps even replace the teacher, who may be needed for other duties.

Based on such preparations, practice of the school plan should be continued until routine procedures have become automatic. Other devices, such as dramatic play, can be used in rehearsing the kinds of behavior that would be appropriate if an alert should occur while the children are not at school. Provision should also be made for acquainting new personnel (students and staff) with the overall plan and for helping each one to understand his own particular role.

Attack Warning

The school civil defense warning system should be coordinated with the city civil defense warning network, and the determination of the mode of transmission and communications should be based on compatibility with overall city warning systems. Among systems in use to transmit civil defense warnings are the telephone, radio, local warning siren system, and the bell-and-lights system.

Civil defense warning recommendations provide for two warning signals:

TAKE COVER—A wailing tone or a series of short blasts on sirens or other sounding devices for a period of 3 minutes. This signal is used to indicate that hostile attack may be imminent and that time permits only the most rapid escape to shelter. In the case of schools, these shelter areas should be predetermined and practice drills should be conducted using the *take cover* signal.

ALERT SIGNAL—A steady sounding of the siren or other warning device for 5 minutes. This signal is used where there is evidence of impending attack and time will permit the orderly action that has been predetermined in this instance. In some areas it will mean evacuation; in others, the mobilization of civil defense forces. The defensive tactics for schools should be predetermined in case of this warning and coordinated with the community civil defense plan. Practice and drill should also be held periodically.

ALL CLEAR—Will not be sounded on public warning devices. Information on the tactical action required will be given by means of public address equipment, radio, or some other voice communication media.

Advance warning of enemy attack may be transmitted to school authorities, depending on the local civil defense plan. Immediately upon receipt of information that enemy attack is imminent, the school sounds its warning devices. Warning signals used in schools should be standardized throughout the system and correspond to local civil defense signals. The alert must be audible in all rooms and recreation areas.

In a civil defense emergency, FM radio and television would go off the air because enemy bombers could "home" on the stations' beams. Only AM radio programs at 640 and 1240 on the radio dial would be in service. By alternate or intermittent broadcasts at reduced power, no one station can serve as a radio beacon for enemy planes. In a civil defense emergency, turn to 640 or 1240 on the AM radio dial for information. Battery radios should be available for use if the regular power supply fails. CONELRAD coverage is limited to urban areas and does not provide rural coverage.

School Shelters

With the realization that millions of children could very well be in school at the time of a nuclear attack, it was imperative that schools take strong steps — supported by local, state, and federal government agencies — to ensure that every school was a safe haven both for children and for the community. In 1959, the Office of Civil and Defense Mobilization published School/Shelter: An Approach to Fallout Protection, *which outlined the requisites not only from a physical perspective, but also from a human perspective.*

The towering mushroom cloud is more than symbol of destruction; it is itself ominous. The myriad particles it bears aloft will drift with the wind and slowly descend — perhaps hundreds of miles from their origin. These particles, perilous until their radioactivity decays, might be visible as they fall through the air, but radiological instruments are needed to determine their degree of danger. A brief exposure to them may cause serious illness. Prolonged exposure could bring death. This is the threat of fallout.

Our great cities and other prime targets face added jeopardy of blast and heat from direct attack but, even within the scope of nuclear warfare, total destruction is a risk to relatively limited areas. A more extensive peril is that of fallout. This danger varies with the size and type of nuclear explosion, with the amount of debris picked up from the surface of the earth, and with meteorological patterns of wind speed and direction. With the differences possible in attack and conditions, we must conclude that even the remotest communities of the United States cannot be considered safe from the hazards of lethal fallout.

To meet the need for protection, there are three possible techniques: evacuation, decontamination, and the building of shelters. Each has its proper place in a balanced program. Since this study deals with the third technique, shelter, it will be considered in some detail. The basic aspect of the shelter procedure is the interposing of a mass of material between shelter occupants and the dangerous radioactive particles.

Fortunately, the delay in deposition of fallout, as it is carried by the winds, could provide a warning period that would enable citizens to reach shelter before being harmed. Government civil defense agencies, utilizing radiological monitoring and meteorological forecasts, will warn citizens of approaching fallout. In circumstances such as this, it is imperative to know what constitutes adequate shelter.

In any locality in the United States, fallout could require shelter occupancy for a period of two weeks or more. This estimate, covering high-grade shelter suitable for protection in heavily contaminated areas and based on the best scientific knowledge, assumes that the shelter is designed to give a protection of 1,000 or more. Inside such a shelter, a person would receive only ¹⁄₁,₀₀₀ of the amount of radiation that he would absorb were he outside the shelter.

Along with education, protection of children always has been a major responsibility of the teaching profession. Various kinds of health and safety programs have become accepted as part of school functions. Training and equipment for emergencies have repeatedly proven their worth for saving lives. Who can number the thousands of children who have been saved by fire alarms and drills, safety patrols, and first aid programs?

In an era faced with the possibility of nuclear attack, every child should be taught the simple rule, "Take cover," but, unless shelter is close at hand, this admonition is inadequate to protect from fallout radiation. A carefully-researched analysis of a suburban Washington, D.C., school district indicated that, in event of an attack on Washington, the school district would likely suffer 52,000 casualties amongst its 84,000 population. With a disaster plan and only 15 minutes warning, it has been predicted that it would be possible to reduce the casualties to 10,000. Statistics such as these have moved school districts in all parts of the country to instigate protection programs. Los Angeles, for example, has designated each one of its school buildings as a protection center. Desirable as such programs may be, the protection they offer is limited. Such shelters seldom provide adequate radiation shielding or the facilities required during an extended shelter occupancy period.

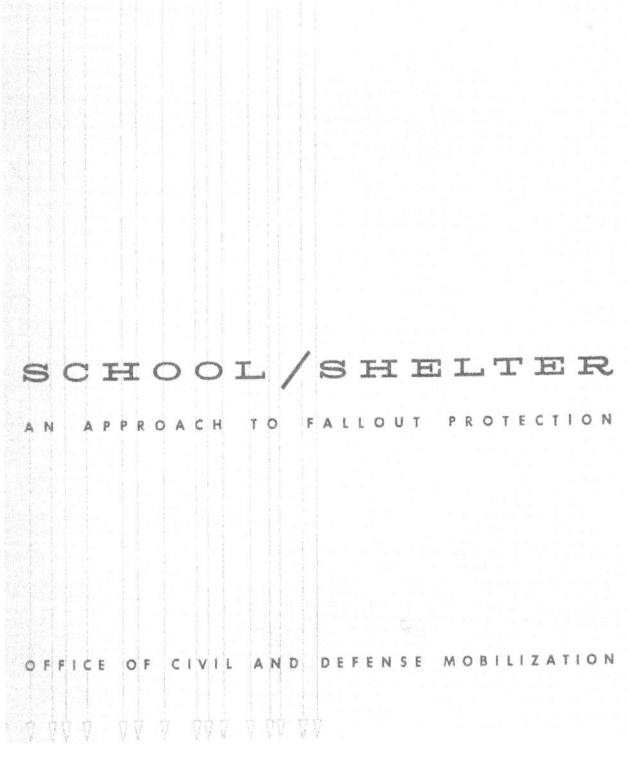

School/Shelter: An Approach to Fallout Protection, Office of Civil and Defense Mobilization, 1959.

Studies and tests have indicated the great potential value of fallout shelters for insuring public safety. Could all of the nation's schools be safeguarded? It is an imposing but not impossible task.

The incorporation of fallout-radiation protection in school buildings is appropriate and advantageous for a number of reasons:

1. Students in elementary, junior high, and high schools comprise nearly one-quarter of the population of the United States. The continued well-being of these youngsters is of extraordinary importance to the future of the nation.

2. Schools are distributed geographically in relationship to concentration of population. Elementary schools, in particular, are closely related to residential population.
3. The school is a permanently established organization with responsible leaders and orderly procedures.
4. The school building is often the most substantial and best-equipped facility in the community.
5. Except for housing, schools are currently the most prevalent building type in the United States. Consequently, shelters in schools provide one of the best opportunities for protection of large numbers of people.

Economy, a prime requisite in school planning, usually rules out separated shelter facilities that are only for emergencies. Normally, it is essential that all sheltered space be available and useful for daily educational purposes. The attempt to combine the ideal school and the ideal shelter creates a number of problems, of which the most conspicuous is that presented by the necessity of surrounding educational spaces with sufficient mass to give radiation protection. In general, this protection requires walls and ceilings of approximately two feet thickness of concrete or equivalent materials. Windows are eliminated and doors are shielded. Obviously, this conflicts with current educational and architectural thinking directed toward achieving teaching spaces of maximum openness and natural light. It is believed by planners, however, that enclosed instructional spaces can be made attractive and comfortable and, in fact, have certain advantages over conventional construction. Among these advantages are better temperature and humidity control, which facilitates the use of air conditioning, and better illumination control, which improves classroom lighting quality and simplifies the use of AV-TV teaching techniques.

Protection Factors

Fundamental to the school/shelter idea is the precept that regular day-to-day life within such a facility would be as school days ought to be everywhere — busy, pleasant, productive. It is impossible to disregard, however, the awful threat these structures were meant to circumvent. What might it be like on the bewildering day when the sirens scream and well-drilled routine propels pupils and teachers to shelter? What might it be like when the sound of the sirens dies away and a prospect of two weeks of confinement and isolation is there to face? No one knows all the answers, but it is apparent that the prospect demands thought, planning, and preparation.

Not only must a school/shelter facility be immediately convertible to shelter use, but it should be operable and habitable as a completely independent entity for a period of approximately two weeks. It must be assumed that, at a time of dire national emergency requiring shelter occupancy, such ordinary services as telephones, water supply, sewage disposal, fuel supply, and food services would be non-functioning or unavailable. Further, that it would be inadvisable for anyone to leave the shelter for any reason during the emergency period. Such a program is very different from ordinary school operation, and the care of shelter occupants under the circumstances described involves diverse physiological and psychological needs.

Among these needs are adequate radiation shielding, nourishing food, pure water, fresh air, sufficient space, disease control, rest and sleep, and morale activities....

Morale Activities

A training program of preparation for shelter occupancy would drill school children in protection techniques and teach them to comprehend a disaster situation. Thus, it is anticipated that most persons entering fallout shelters would not have suffered prior psychic trauma. It is expected that most emotional problems would be caused by such shelter conditions as confinement, overcrowding, rationing of food and water, monotony, and possible separation from families. Children are emotionally resilient, and most will prove adaptable. It is estimated, however, that four to eight percent may suffer major emotional upsets — aggravations, for the most part, of normal instabilities. Such reactions can have a contagious effect, and special provision should be made for isolation and care of these individuals. Less strong disturbance among a large number of children may take the form of irritability, or acts of aggression. Children of elementary school age respond more favorably to stressful situations if they are able to meet them in familiar social and physical surroundings. For this reason, it is believed there are advantages in retaining, where possible, the existing school pattern of group relationships and activities. This suggests the desirability of several separated groups within a single shelter.

Probably the best morale activity during a two week shelter occupancy would be a normal educational program, but such a program would be difficult to maintain. Even using a double shift, with half the children sleeping while half are awake, the typical sheltered classroom probably would be filled to more than double its normal occupancy. This crowding, coupled with the day long schedule of shelter confinement, implies extraordinary demands on teacher capabilities, and suggests increased use of large group activities. An important part of a shelter program would be recreation, active and passive. School children of elementary school age have an essential urge to move about. An unobstructed space should be provided within a shelter where groups of children can, for short periods of time, participate in active play. Similarly, a necessary part of shelter provisions will be the passive recreation equipment needed to make endurable a two week confinement.

Part 6

Find Shelter

You and Civil Defense, Civil Defense Commission, State of New York, no date.

Survival Requirements

On May 7, 1958, the federal government announced the National Policy on Shelters, which formalized the government's official role in protecting the American people. Leo A. Hoegh, director of the Office of Civil and Defense Mobilization, described the new policy in Individual and Family Survival Requirements, *published by his office in 1959.*

National Policy on Shelters

The Administration has conducted exhaustive studies and tests with respect to protective measures to safeguard our citizens against the effects of nuclear weapons. These several analyses have indicated that there is a great potential for the saving of life by fallout shelters. In the event of nuclear attack on this country, fallout shelters offer the best single nonmilitary defense measure for the protection of the greatest number of people.

Furthermore, a nation with adequate fallout protection is a nation which would be more difficult to successfully attack. This fact alone would substantially lesson the temptation of an aggressor to launch an attack.

The Administration's national civil defense policy, which now includes planning for the movement of people from target areas if time permits, will now also include the use of shelters to provide protection from radioactive fallout.

To implement this established policy, the Administration will undertake the following action:

1. The Administration will bring to every American all of the facts as to the possible effects of nuclear attack, and inform him of the steps which he and his State and local governments can take to minimize such effects.

The present civil defense programs for information and education will therefore be substantially expanded in order to acquaint the people with the fallout hazard and how to effectively overcome it. The public education program will include information on:

(a) Nuclear weapons' effects on people, plants, and animals;

(b) The provision of effective fallout protection, how to construct a fallout shelter, and how to improvise effective shelter;

(c) Necessary measures for the protection of food and water;

(d) How to carry out radiological decontamination; and

(e) What governments — Federal, State, and local — are themselves doing about fallout protection.

2. **The Administration will initiate a survey of existing structures on a sampling basis, in order to assemble definite information on the capabilities of existing structures to provide fallout shelter, particularly in larger cities.**
Many facilities, such as existing buildings, mines, subways, tunnels, cyclone cellars, etc., already afford some fallout protection. Action will be taken to accurately determine the protection afforded by all such facilities in order to make maximum use of them.

3. **The Administration will accelerate research in order to show how fallout shelters may be incorporated in existing, as well as in new, buildings**—whether in homes, other private buildings, or governmental structures. Designs of shelters will be perfected to assure the most economic and effective types.

4. **The Administration will construct a limited number of prototype shelters of various kinds, suitable to different geographical and climatic areas.** These will be tested by actual occupancy by differing numbers of people for realistic periods of time. They will also have practical peacetime uses. Some of the prototype structures will be incorporated in:

(a) Underground parking garages.
(b) Understreet shelters.
(c) Subways.
(d) The Federal highway program—patrol and maintenance facilities.
(e) Additions to existing schools and new schools, including such facilities as cafeterias, assembly space, and classrooms.
(f) Additions to existing hospitals and new hospitals, including such facilities as cafeterias, visitors' and convalescent rooms, and reserve areas.
(g) Industrial plants.
(h) Commercial buildings.
(i) Family residences and apartments, including such facilities as bathrooms, garages, basements, and recreation rooms.

5. **The Administration will provide leadership and example by incorporating fallout shelters in appropriate new Federal buildings hereafter designed for civilian use.**
Federal example is an indispensable element to stimulate

APPENDIX 1
(ANNEX 2 - INDIVIDUAL ACTION)

Individual and Family Survival Requirements

NP-2-1
NATIONAL PLAN APPENDIX SERIES

Executive Office of the President
OFFICE OF CIVIL AND DEFENSE MOBILIZATION

Individual and Family Survival Requirements, Office of Civil and Defense Mobilization, 1959.

State, local government, and private investment for fallout shelters. Community use of shelters in these new buildings is contemplated.

There will be no massive federally financed shelter construction program.

With reference to blast shelters, there are still difficult questions having to do with the amount of time that would be available to enter the shelters, the uncertainty of missile accuracy, and the effectiveness of our active defense. There is no assurance that even the deepest shelter would give protection to a sufficient number of people to justify the cost. In addition, there may not be sufficient warning time in view of the development of missile capabilities to permit the effective use of blast shelters.

Our chief deterrent to war will continue to be our active military capability. Our active military defense may eventually have the capability of effectively preventing an enemy from striking intended targets. Highest priority is to be given to the development of this capability.

Common prudence requires that the Federal Government take steps to assist each American to prepare himself—as he would through insurance—against any disaster to meet a possible—although unwanted—eventuality. The national shelter policy is founded upon this principle.

This approach will provide the stimulation necessary for the American people to make preparations for fallout protection. The Federal Government will also work with State and local governments and with private industries to expedite and facilitate the provision of fallout shelter.

The Administration believes that when the American people fully understand the problem that confronts them, they will rise to meet the challenge, as they have invariably done in the past. This is particularly true now that the national policy has been declared, backed up with Federal example, Federal leadership, and Federal guidance. The President has directed me to put this policy into effect.

Protection of our people is not new in the United States. When a free America was being built by our forebears, every log cabin and every dwelling had a dual purpose — namely, a home and a fortress. Today, the citizen should be called upon to make the same contribution as our forebears — not for building a free America, but for sustaining a free America.

Top: This family is building a basement compact shelter of sand-filled concrete blocks. *Bottom:* This backyard plywood shelter can be built partially above ground and mounded over with earth, or be built totally below ground level (*Fallout Protection*, Department of Defense, Office of Civil Defense, 1961).

Shelter Suppliess 151

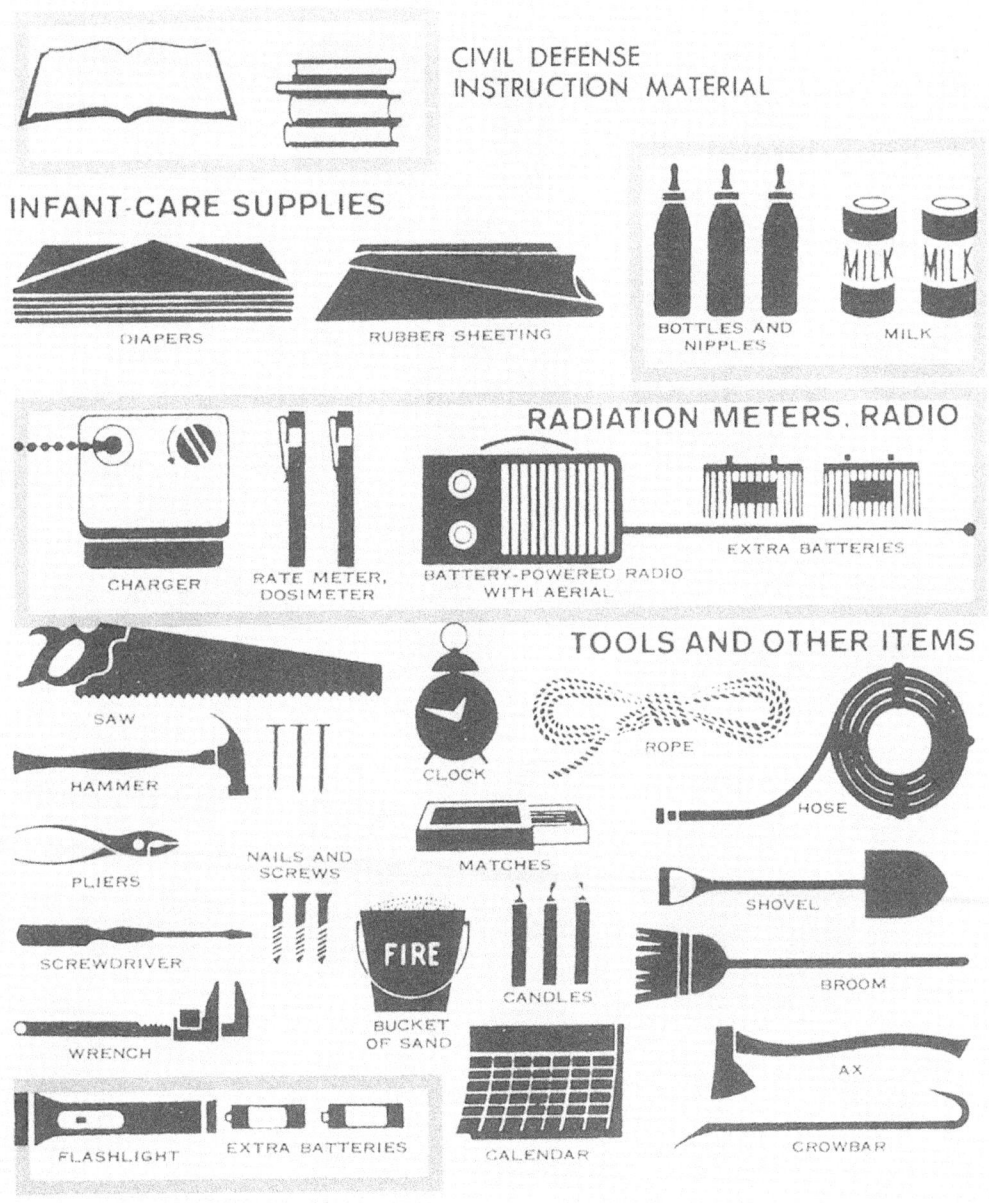

Every shelter needed the essentials, from sanitation supplies and food, to radiation meters and emergency toilets. The supplies listed on this page and on page 152 were recommended in *Fallout Protection*, published by the Department of Defense, Office of Civil Defense in 1961.

Shelter from Fallout

Every citizen who was serious about surviving a nuclear attack had a copy of The Family Fallout Shelter, *published by the Office of Civil and Defense Mobilization in 1959. The booklet included blueprints for a variety of shelters and explained why you needed one.*

Fallout Shelter Is Needed Everywhere

One thing is certain if this country is attacked with nuclear weapons: our air and missile bases will be primary targets.

The enemy would try to knock out our retaliatory power.

He might also try to destroy our cities.

No one can be sure now how far the enemy will go.

But it must be emphasized that even if an enemy confines his attack to our retaliatory bases, the radioactive fallout from his nuclear bombs would threaten life in the entire country. An atomic burst on the ground sends up a mushroom cloud from which radioactive dust will fall hundreds of miles away.

Fallout from one test explosion spread over 7,000 square miles of the Pacific Ocean.

The following maps show the spread of fallout after a large assumed attack on military and civilian targets. Hour by hour the fallout spreads and overlaps until, after 24 hours, it almost completely covers the nation. (See Figures 1 and 2.)

These maps show where the wind would have carried the fallout from the assumed attack on a given day. On another day, the wind could swing in any other direction and turn safe areas on these maps into areas of extreme fallout danger.

The fallout radiation threat indicated on the map is not uniform. The danger diminishes as the fallout drifts further from the points of nuclear explosion. But even on the extreme limits of the drift, the fallout remains a menace to life and health for some time.

The lesson is: fallout shelter is needed everywhere.

The radioactivity of fallout decays rapidly at first. *Forty-nine hours after an atomic burst, the radiation intensity is only about 1 percent of what it was an hour after the explosion. But the radiation may be so intense at the start that 1 percent may be extremely dangerous.*

Therefore, civil defense instructions received over CONELRAD or by other means should be followed. A battery-powered radio is essential. When radiation meters suitable for home use are available, they will be of value in locating that portion of the home

Part 6—Find Shelter

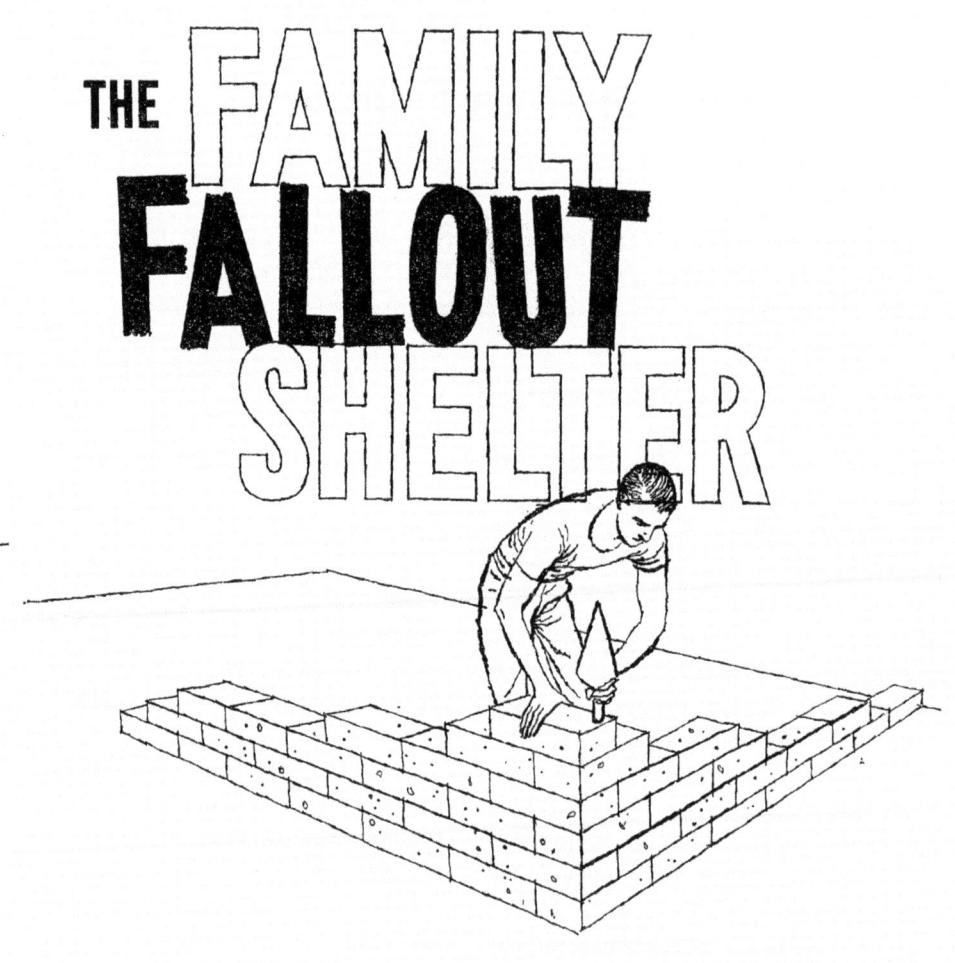

THE FAMILY FALLOUT SHELTER

MP-15

A committee of the National Academy of Sciences, in a recent study of national preparedness, concluded:

> "*Adequate shielding is the only effective means of preventing radiation casualties.*"

OFFICE OF CIVIL AND DEFENSE MOBILIZATION

The Family Fallout Shelter, Office of Civil and Defense Mobilization, 1959.

Shelter from Fallout

Figure 1: Fallout areas at one hour after detonation.

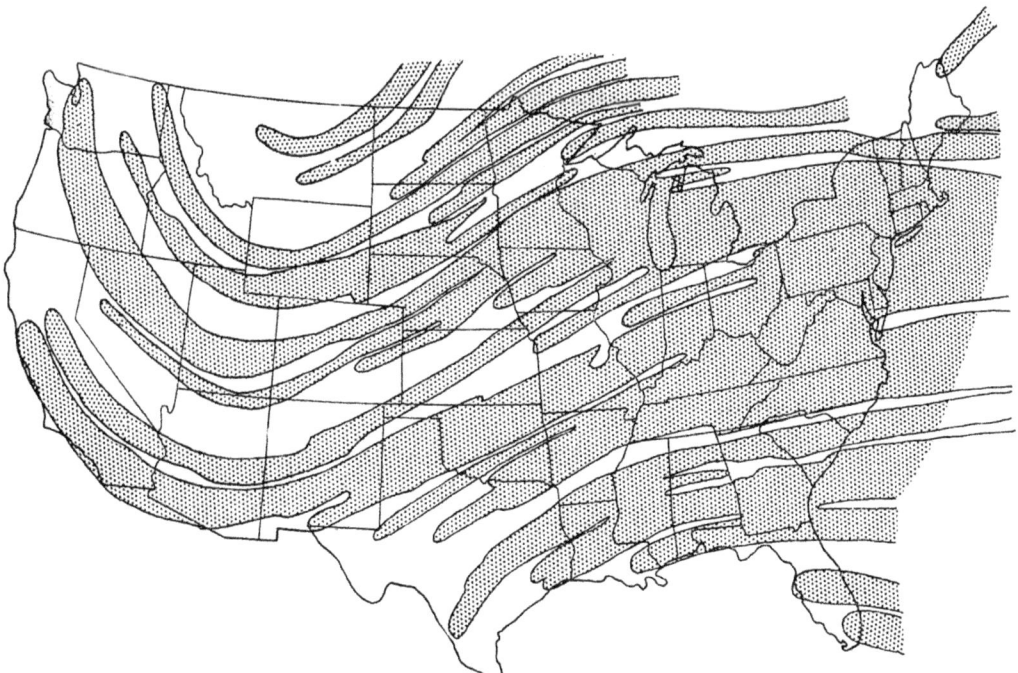

Figure 2: Fallout areas at 24 hours after detonation.

which offers the best protection against fallout radiation. There is a possibility that battery-powered radios with built-in radiation meters may become available. One instrument thus would serve both purposes.

Your local civil defense will gather its own information and will receive broad information from State and Federal sources. It will tell you as soon as possible:

- How long to stay in your shelter.
- How soon you may go outdoors.
- How long you may stay outside.

You should be prepared to stay in your shelter full time for at least several days and to make it your home for 14 days or longer. Families with children will have particular problems. They should provide for simple recreation.

There should be a task for everyone and these tasks should be rotated. Part of the family should be sleeping while the rest is awake.

To break the monotony, it may be necessary to invent tasks that will keep the family busy. Records such as diaries can be kept.

The survival of the family will depend largely on information received by radio. A record should be kept of the information and instructions, including the time and date of broadcast.

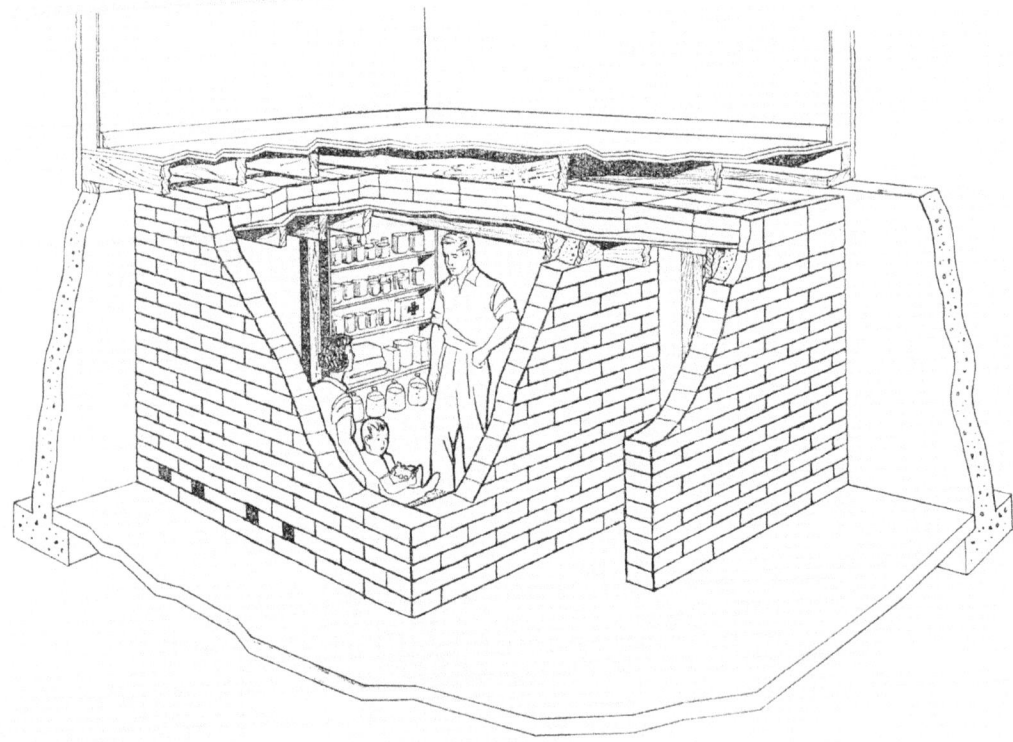

Basement shelters were among the least expensive types that could still provide substantial protection from an atomic blast. This concrete block shelter placed in the corner of a basement provided ambitious families with a do-it-yourself project that might mean their very survival.

Family rationing probably will be necessary.

Blowers should be operated periodically on a regular schedule.

There will come a time in a basement shelter when the radiation has decayed enough to allow use of the whole basement. However, as much time as possible should be spent within the shelter to hold radiation exposure to a minimum.

The housekeeping problems of living in a shelter will begin as soon as the shelter is occupied. Food, medical supplies, utensils, and equipment, if not already stored in the shelter, must be quickly gathered up and carried into it.

After the family has settled in the shelter, the housekeeping rules should be spelled out by the adult in charge.

Sanitation in the confines of the family shelter will require much thought and planning.

Provision for emergency toilet facilities and disposal of human wastes will be an unfamiliar problem. A covered container such as a kitchen garbage pail might do as a toilet. A 10-gallon garbage can, with a tightly fitting cover, could be used to keep the wastes until it is safe to leave the shelter.

Water rationing will be difficult and should be planned carefully.

A portable electric heater is advisable for shelters in cold climates. It would take the chill from the shelter in the beginning. Even if the electric power fails after an attack, any time that the heater has been used will make the shelter that much more comfortable. Body heat in the close quarters will help keep up the temperature. Warm clothing and bedding, of course, are essential.

Open-flame heating or cooking should be avoided. A flame would use up air.

Some families already have held weekend rehearsals in their home shelters to learn the problems and to determine for themselves what supplies they would need.

Shelter Preparation

Although evacuation was the best way to survive a nuclear attack, everyone might not have time to evacuate—which meant preparing a home shelter, just in case. Home Protection Exercises, *originally published in November 1953 by the Federal Civil Defense Administration and revised in 1957, offered instructions and recommended exercises for the family dedicated to civil defense preparation.*

With the development of more powerful nuclear weapons, evacuation has become the best defense against the blast and fire resulting from the explosion of these weapons. However, to be successful there must be sufficient warning time for evacuation, and sufficient warning time cannot be assured for everyone.

In many cases, the construction of family shelters against the blast and heat effects of large nuclear weapons would be impracticable because of building and cost factors. Family shelters against nuclear radiation—radioactive fallout—*are* practicable and will be needed no matter where you live because harmful radioactive fallout can occur hundreds of miles from the explosion of a large nuclear weapon.

A family shelter against radioactive fallout has an added advantage for those who live in the "tornado belt" of the country, because it can serve equally well as refuge and protection from the devastation caused by these violent storms.

Procedure

1. The following should be considered in choosing the site and type of construction of your home shelter against fallout radiation:
    a. For lower cost, choose a corner in your basement, bearing in mind that if the shelter is to double as protection against tornadoes, the southwest corner is the most desirable. The shelter should be strong enough to support the debris load if your house should collapse, and should have enough shielding material around and over it to reduce the penetration of nuclear radiation to safe levels.
    b. If your house does not have a basement or if it is not feasible to build a basement shelter, you can build at a little greater cost an outside underground shelter. Choose a site for your underground shelter that will not be covered by debris if your house should be blown down. The more earth cover the better, up to a maximum of 3 feet.

Home Protection Exercises, Office of Civil and Defense Mobilization, 1953, revised 1957.

c. If the water level in the ground is too high, an aboveground shelter may be built. This shelter could also be used as a toolhouse or storage shed.

2. You will have to decide which type shelter will best suit your family needs — a basement corner room shelter, or an outside shelter. Building the family shelter may be done by a contractor or by members of the family. As a family project, one person should act as construction superintendent, and other members of the family should serve as helpers.

3. You will need some kind of emergency lighting because electric power often fails first in a disaster. Keep a flashlight in your shelter.

4. Since radio will be your immediate source of official information and instructions (640 and 1240 kc. on your standard AM radio dial), you should label these on your radio dial now.

The broadcasting industry and the Government, working together, have devised a special system of AM (Standard) radio broadcasting to bring you official word on what to do in time of emergency.

The system is officially entitled "Plan for CONtrol of ELectromagnetic RADiations"—CONELRAD for short.

Under the CONELRAD emergency broadcasting system, you will be able to receive radio programs originating from three different sources — local, state, and national. Programs originating locally will be broadcast direct. Line connections are arranged for programs originating on a state or regional basis. By using the existing network structures and line connections between stations, officials can broadcast programs which will reach most of the country.

You will not be able to use your regular radio if electric power is cut off, so it is wise to have a portable, battery-operated radio which can be taken to your shelter. You should also have extra batteries for your radio.

5. You should have a first-aid kit in or near your shelter.

6. You should have a 2-week supply of food and water on hand for emergency use. Probably you have a partial supply of food in your refrigerator and cupboards. You should add a stock of canned and dried foods that can be eaten without cooking, such as soups and juices, fish, milk, and meat. Avoid foods that would increase thirst. Store this emergency food in your evacuation kit or near the family shelter.

Your emergency supplies should include drinking water in bottles or jars, packed to avoid breakage. Store at least 7 gallons for each member of the family. Remember that milk, fruit, juices, and bottled beverages can also be used. Water-packed fruits and vegetables also will give you extra liquids for emergency drinking purposes. Another source is your hot water heater, which usually will provide 30 or 60 gallons of water, depending on the size of the tank.

7. Other needed supplies which should be in or near your shelter include blankets, warm clothes for cold weather, pliers or a wrench, heavy gloves, paper cups and plates, eating utensils, extra bulbs and batteries for your flashlight and portable radio, a supply of old newspapers, toilet tissue, sanitary napkins, invalid supplies if you have illness in the house, and disposable diapers if you have a baby. Also provide escape tools such as a pick, shovel, crowbar, or ax.

You also should have available spare washcloths, towels, soap, matches, a can opener, one or more cooking utensils, a small compact cooking unit, a small covered pail or can for human waste, and a supply of paper sacks for making soil bags.

A chart should be posted in the family shelter showing exact location of each item of emergency supplies and tools.

Practice

1. Assemble your family and discuss the need for a shelter and emergency supplies. Make sure everyone understands why they are needed and how they are to be used.

2. After assigning the various shelter needs to responsible members of your family, set a time limit for carrying out each assignment.

3. Hold another family meeting on the specified date and check your shelter provisions against the prescribed items. If anything is missing, set a deadline for obtaining it and storing it in its proper place.

4. Check the list again at the deadline date and make sure everyone understands where the required items are stored and who is to get them to the shelter in an emergency — if it is not practical to store them in the shelter. Review how they are to be used.

BEFORE DISASTER STRIKES

YOU SHOULD KNOW....

Where to find safe water

How to turn off water service valve

How to purify water

What foods to store and how to prepare them

What foods are unsafe

How to dispose of garbage

How to dispose of human wastes

How to make soil bags

What to do with frozen foods

BEFORE DISASTER STRIKES

YOU SHOULD HAVE....

- Stored water or other liquid (7 gals. per person)
- A 2-week supply of proper foods, paper plates and napkins
- Cooking and eating utensils, measuring cup, can and bottle openers, pocket knife and matches
- Special foods for babies and the sick
- Large garbage can to keep garbage
- Smaller can for human wastes

A covered pail for bathroom purposes

Toilet tissue, paper towels, sanitary napkins, disposable diapers, soap

Rubber sheeting and special equipment for the sick

Grocery bags, week's supply of newspapers for sanitary uses, waterproof gloves

2 pts. of household chlorine, 1 qt. of 5 percent DDT

Wrench, screwdriver, shovel, and other tools

Opposite and above: Emergency Sanitation at Home, Office of Civil and Defense Mobilization, 1958.

Know How to Survive

Knowing the dangers of nuclear attack was not enough; Americans also needed to know how best to survive, such as which type of shelter to build. The 1960 brochure, Ten for Survival: Survive Nuclear Attack, *published by the Office of Civil and Defense Mobilization, covered the major effects of nuclear bombs and then suggested a variety of possible shelter designs.*

To protect yourself at the time of a nuclear explosion, you must understand NOW the hazards you would face.

You probably will be warned in advance by siren or radio that attack is coming. The Air Force, with its far-flung detection network, and the Office of Civil and Defense Mobilization are working together to do everything possible to warn you.

But surprise attack could come. You must know what to do if it does.

YOU SHOULD KNOW THE
THREE MAIN DESTRUCTIVE EFFECTS OF A
NUCLEAR EXPLOSION.
HEAT, BLAST, FALLOUT.

Heat

Dangers facing you: The bomb produces heat of several million degrees — a good deal hotter than the temperature on the surface of the sun. This heat travels at the speed of light. A megaton explosion could kill an unshielded man 8 miles from ground zero. A 20-megaton explosion could kill an unshielded man 20 miles away. It could blister and cripple the bodies of unsheltered people well beyond that.

What you should do: Beyond the 5-mile radius of total destruction, but still within range of the immediate killing power of the bomb, you would have split seconds to save your life.

You would have to act with instinctive speed to take cover behind whatever was at hand.

Blast

Dangers facing you: The shock waves of blast from a nuclear explosion travel about 900 miles an hour — nine times the force of a major hurricane! Blast could destroy a brick building 9½ miles from ground zero.

What you should do: If caught unprotected beyond the 5-mile circle of destruction, you could save your life with an instantaneous dive for cover.

Cover is the same for both heat and blast.

In open country it might be a ditch or culvert. Lie face down and stay there until the heat and blast waves have passed.

In the city it might be a wall, a building, or even a truck.

Indoors it would be the floor (behind furniture or as close to an inside wall as possible).

THE MAIN IDEA — GET BEHIND SOMETHING

Fallout

Dangers facing you: The millions of tons of pulverized earth and debris sucked up as high as 15 miles by the fireball of a large nuclear explosion become a deadly radioactive fallout cloud. It spreads its lethal radioactivity over wide areas, hundreds of miles downwind from ground zero. Fallout radioactivity cannot be detected by taste or touch. Sometimes, but not always, the fine ash or dust carrying the radioactivity is visible. It fills the atmosphere, the air you breathe, and attacks the vital organs of your body with invisible radiation.

Ten for Survival: Survive Nuclear Attack, Office of Civil and Defense Mobilization, 1960.

Protection from Fallout

The best protection against fallout radiation is a fallout shelter. Every family should have one. It can be an area in a building of such heavy construction as to afford the required shielding or a shelter designed to be a unit of a family dwelling.

Basement Concrete Block Shelter, designed as a do-it-yourself project. Solid concrete blocks are used to build it.

Underground Concrete Shelters, one designed as a basement shelter in new housing, and one as an outdoor, underground shelter.

Preshaped Metal Shelter, built by placing preshaped corrugated metal sections on or close to the surface of the ground and mounding them over with earth.

Aboveground Double-Wall Shelter, which is a double-walled, concrete block structure with the walls built nearly 2 feet apart. The space between the walls is filled with earth. A roof is built of either poured concrete or wood and covered with earth.

THESE SHELTERS WILL PROVIDE YOU WITH EXCELLENT PROTECTION.

If you are caught by fallout away from a shelter or have no shelter in your home, the best place to be in order of the protection you would get would be:

1. In a corner of a basement.
2. In the center of the basement.
   (Sandbags covering basement windows will increase protection.)
3. First floor inside hallway of a two-story house.
4. Inside hallway of a one-story house.

Shelter in Apartment Buildings

Apartment buildings generally provide more fallout protection than houses.

The central area of the ground floor of an apartment building provides good shelter. The subsurface basement of a heavy apartment building might give as much fallout protection as a concrete block shelter in the basement of a house.

If your fallout shelter is to be an apartment house basement, you should survey it in advance to assure that there is ventilation, water, lighting, and the other requirements of a prepared shelter. You would probably have time to carry your family supplies from your apartment to the basement after an attack warning before any fallout arrives. If not, a quick trip from the basement to your apartment to get supplies is not likely to present any significant additional hazard.

If We Are Bombed: A Handbook for Your Protection, St. Paul (Minn.) Civil Defense, no date.

Part 7

Evacuate

Home Protection Exercises, Federal Civil Defense Administration, 1953.

Highways for Civil Defense

On June 29, 1956, President Dwight D. Eisenhower signed the National Interstate and Defense Highways Act, which called for $25 billion to construct 41,000 miles of interstate highways over a 20-year period. The previous year, in September 1955, however, the Bureau of Public Roads initiated a study on "the capabilities of rural and suburban streets and highways for carrying out evacuation of 185 urban areas identified by the Federal Civil Defense Administration as potential targets." The National Interstate and Defense Highways Act, in fact, was enacted not only to improve the highway system, but also to improve the ability to evacuate urban areas in case of nuclear attack. The following is an excerpt of this study.

The Problem

Briefly expressed, the problem under consideration is one of survival of populations in urban centers if subjected to enemy attack. Three significant factors have been instrumental in establishing the dimensions of the problem; evaluation of these factors is required in any rational analysis of the data. These factors involve the present and future development of:

1. Nuclear weapons with their enlarged areas of destruction and radioactive fallout potentialities.

2. Means of delivery of the bomb by air, submarine, or clandestine methods.

3. Means of defense against delivery of the bomb, with the related factor of expected warning time to large population centers for possible evacuation programs.

Consideration of these three items in relation to the civil defense problem of the 185 target areas under consideration in this study indicates that:

1. The potential area of severe bomb blast is such as to make target areas almost wholly subject to first degree effects with severe problems of radioactive fallout in certain adjoining areas.

2. Urban centers would be vulnerable to attack on a total war basis, with greater vulnerability along the coastal areas.

3. Warning time would be short. Estimates released by the Federal Civil Defense Administration indicate from 1½ hours warning at border and coastal cities to 3 or 4 hours for cities in the interior of the country. The probability exists that developments in methods of delivery and detection have altered or may soon alter this factor of warning time, either increasing or decreasing it.

Purpose of the Study

In consideration of the conditions presently constituting the broad civil defense problem, it is the purpose of this study to determine on a nationwide basis:

1. The adequacy of the present highway and street systems in rural and suburban areas to permit evacuation of urban populations by motor vehicles.

2. The extent that roadway improvements in these areas would permit faster or more complete evacuation of urban populations, and the estimated cost of such improvements.

3. The relationship between normal highway construction programs and increase in roadway capacity for evacuation purposes.

Conclusions

The problems of civil defense are many and complex, and although this study constitutes a preliminary analysis of only one element of the problem, the significance of the findings cannot be obviated in the light of present day weapons and their means of delivery, nor should they be disregarded in consideration of weaponry development that may ensue in the next decade. It is obvious that the primary importance of the study is intimately correlated with the time factor—time to precondition the public fully to undertake an orderly evacuation, time to construct dispersal areas or shelters, and time to add capacity to road systems to permit greater or faster evacuation of possible target areas if such a policy were decided upon.

It is necessary before considering the significance of the factual information to have a full understanding of the purposes and governing conditions of the study. The three basic objectives of the study are to measure the capabilities of the present highway system to accomplish evacuation of the designated FCDA target areas; estimate to a reasonable degree the extent and cost that highway improvements would permit faster or more complete evacuation of urban populations to the limits of full evacuation; and establish the relationship of normal construction programs to an increased capability of the road systems for evacuation purposes.

In establishing any conclusions from the data, it is desirable to point out that this report represents only a preliminary analysis of the factual information. It is desirable that the basic information should be more thoroughly examined, and, if necessary, additional relationships of highway capacity, improvement costs, and evacuation distances and time requirements should be developed. Adjustments for population changes should also be reflected for future years.

In measuring the capabilities of the present road systems, the most significant finding of the study is the fact that approximately 32 million people of the 90.7 million in the 185 target areas could possibly be evacuated to a 15-mile distance from a selected ground zero in 1½ hours by motor vehicle under conditions that would place the roads under full capacity operations within a reasonably short time after warning. This, of course, would be dependent upon full preconditioning of the population for evacuation and efficient traffic operations. Equally important is the finding that total evacuation of most large urban areas over present street and highway systems within reasonable warning time is impossible. This does not imply that large numbers of people could not be removed from the target areas, but it does prove that when warning times are short additional means of survival must be considered for these places. In addition, evacuation to this distance would in no manner insure the civilian population against the possible effects of radioactive fallout. The data reveal that estimated expenditures for increasing highway and street capacity to carry out *total* evacuation of 159 target areas to the 25-mile screenline in 2 hours approaches $20 billion. To accomplish such construction would require an extended period of time during which population increases could alter capacity requirements. Upon completion of such construction, possible reactions of the public on receipt of an alert might also be such as to question the utilization of this capacity to anywhere near maximum. No program involving large expenditures for civilian defense against presently known weapons should be adopted without weighing its effectiveness against weapons that may be developed in the not too distant future.

A realistic approach to the problems in these areas would appear to require considerations of a combined shelter-evacuation plan, with further study of the relationships of the two elements based upon survival plan studies now under way.

Examination of the normal highway needs development by the State highway departments and correlated by the U.S. Bureau of Public Roads, indicates that within a 10-year period one-sixth of the additional highway capacity required for total evacuation of the 185 target areas to a 15-mile distance from ground zero might be obtained.

Omitting for the moment the exigencies of the present situation in relation to weaponry development and civil defense, the longer range policies for dispersal of industry and reduction of urban vulnerability are intimately related to highway and roadway construction.... Present highway programs with Federal emphasis upon the interstate system should greatly encourage the implementation of these programs without undue changes in the economic structure of the areas involved. Factual studies on land use arising from new highway developments have shown that high-type limited access highways provide a measure of direction in selecting sites for industrial development or expansion, as well as residential growth....

In the final analysis, if the true value of the material presented in this report is to be used to develop a policy which would incorporate the use of highway facilities for evacuation purposes, an intensive study of the elements of weaponry development and delivery must be made. Such study should at least consider the full effects of the following developments that could influence the need or practicability of evacuation:

1. Probable size with blast damage and thermal effects of nuclear weapons.

2. Related radioactive fallout effects connected with weaponry development.

3. Consideration of techniques for target annihilation, especially in view of increased stockpiles of nuclear weapons.

4. Developments in means of delivery by aircraft, guided missiles, and intercontinental ballistic missiles, with due consideration to the present situation of guided missile development with increasing range and adaptability for launching from submarines.

5. The types and degree of effectiveness of defense that may be developed against these weapons.

If the development of weaponry and modes of attack will (1) reduce the warning time and (2) increase the area and degree of destructiveness and increase the areas made untenable through covering of greater areas with fallout, the effectiveness of evacuation following warning of enemy attack would be greatly reduced.

Analysis of the problem based upon public testimony of experts in the field of weaponry development and the material evaluated in this preliminary study indicates and emphasizes the necessity for a consideration of a combination of evacuation and shelter in order that the greatest degree of protection for the civilian population of this country may be obtained.

The civil defense problems of the nation are intimately related to the present road systems and to the expansion and development of these systems in the future. Looking at the longer range problems, the accelerated program of highway and street construction, if maintained, should provide a sound base for increasing the potentialities for possible survival in the atomic age in addition to the great benefits derived from normal economic growth and development of one of the most important national assets in deterring aggression — industrial capacity.

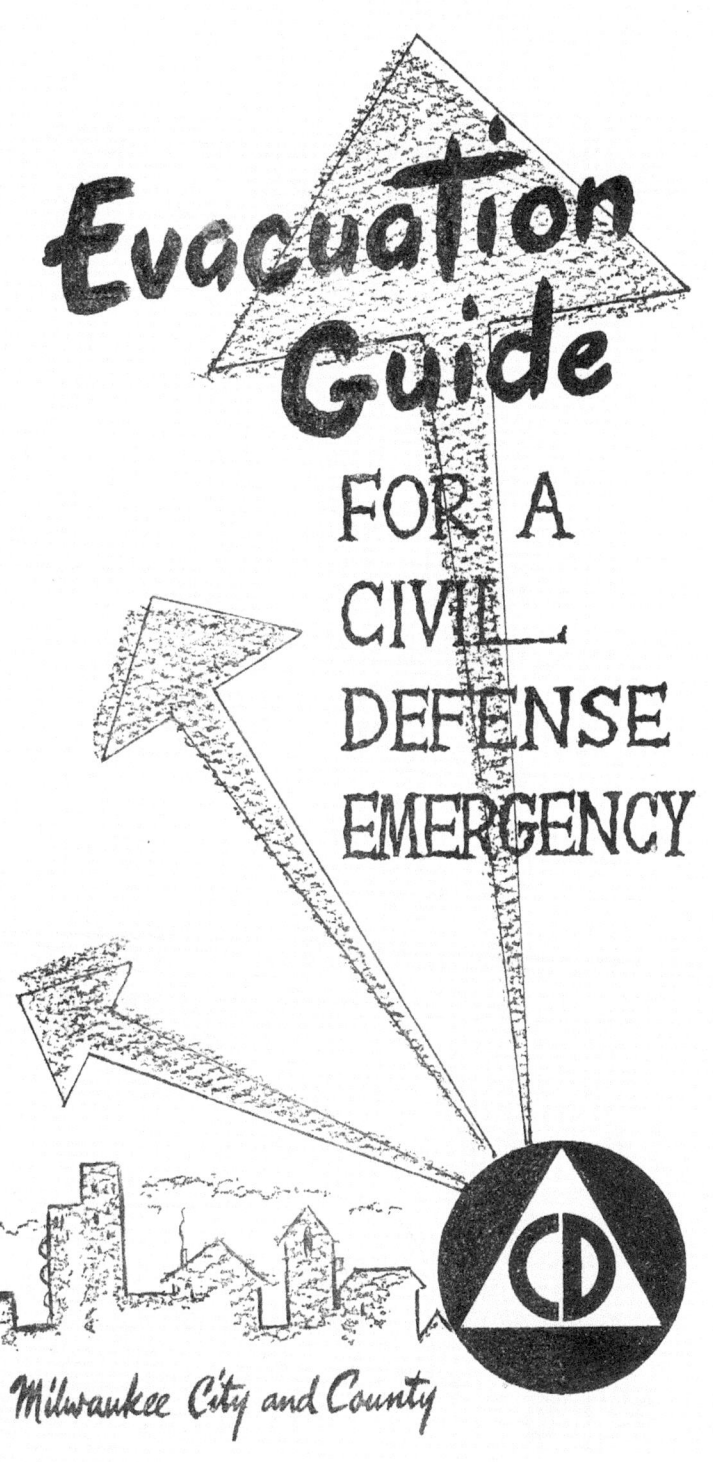

Evacuation Guide for a Civil Defense Emergency, Milwaukee City Civil Defense Administration, no date.

REMEMBER....

1. It can happen here.
2. If it does, distance from the target area (the city) is your surest protection.
3. The chances are good that you will have time to get out. Anyway, CONELRAD (640 or 1240 kilocycles, on AM radio sets) will tell you how much time there is. You should have a battery-powered radio in case of a power failure.
4. There are only two signals. A long, uninterrupted blast of the sirens for several minutes is the Alert Signal. A sharp rising and falling of the sirens is the Take Cover Signal. Turn on your radio to 640 or 1240. During an alert, only civil defense sirens will be sounded. All fire and police departments, ambulance and other sirens will be silenced.
5. Have your family plan what to do under various conditions. Then do it calmly.
6. Work off the top half of the gas tank in your car. Save the bottom half for emergencies.
7. Drive with care. A slight accident that disables your car could be fatal to you, your family and many others under these conditions. Keep your car radio tuned to the CONELRAD frequencies, 640 or 1240.
8. Turn off the evacuation route only after you get permission from traffic police and are well beyond the safety line.
9. If you have no car, walk to an evacuation route and keep walking out until picked up.
10. Study the map, on opposite side, know your CD area. Have a family civil defense test exercise.
11. Facts about fallout are important. Keep calm. Take cover.
12. Know your Home Defense Officer. She will help you plan, arrange transportation and know where to go, how to get there and what to take.
13. Though it may not happen, it can happen here, and the future of your family and your country may depend on what you do about it.

 **MILWAUKEE CIVIL DEFENSE ADMINISTRATION**

(Credit is extended to the St. Louis City-County Civil Defense organization for originating the pattern for this pamphlet).

Evacuation Guide for a Civil Defense Emergency, Milwaukee City Civil Defense Administration, no date.

Will to Survive

Although fallout shelters were still encouraged, at home and in the community, the hydrogen bomb—1,000 times more powerful than an atomic bomb—made evacuation a better tactic for survival by the mid–1950s. Will to Survive, *published by the Ohio Valley Civil Defense Authority in 1955, emphasized the necessity of being knowledgeable and self-reliant.*

When any disaster comes, self-help is essential. Organized aid from Civil Defense authorities cannot possibly assist each individual immediately.

For you as an individual, self-reliance is the quickest, surest means to survival. KNOW HOW to help yourself by knowing this portion of the official OHIO VALLEY CIVIL DEFENSE AUTHORITY plan for all of the Cincinnati Metropolitan area. The plan is a simple, common-sense means to survival. It is in complete agreement and coordination with State and Federal policy.

It's Your Life

Your survival in disaster depends on you. **Now** is the time you and your family must inform yourselves. Make your decisions and determine individual action. This is the best way to insure survival.

When a Civil Defense siren sounds, you either take the best cover or shelter, or you evacuate the area, according to the siren signals and CONELRAD.

Will to Survive, Ohio Valley Civil Defense Authority, 1955.

Part 7 — Evacuate

To Take Shelter When Attacked Without Warning

Your first indication of a nuclear attack when no warning siren sounds will be a very brilliant flash — the brightest you've ever seen. This will be followed by a heavy shock wave, the time interval between the flash and shock depends upon your distance from the center of the explosion. In that interval (probably a few seconds), if you are indoors dive under the nearest heavy piece of furniture or counter, or, if there is none available, lie flat on the floor, face down, alongside a wall and out of line with windows to avoid flying glass.

If in an automobile, park at the nearest curb and crouch face down on the floor of car. Protect your face, head, and neck with your arms.

If outdoors, lie flat on the ground, face down, and cover your head and neck with your arms. A ditch, a gutter, the side of a wall, or even a curb will give partial shielding. By lying down flat, you double your chance for survival. Immediately after the shock wave has passed, get into the best available shelter.

**DON'T TRY TO GO ANY PLACE IN PARTICULAR
JUST GET OUT
FOLLOW THE CD SIGNS AND TRAFFIC LIGHTS
AND THE LARGEST NUMBER OF PEOPLE
WILL ESCAPE**

To Evacuate

When the warning comes and all people within the danger area are told to leave, get into or on some kind of vehicle — any kind of vehicle, including railroad trains, and move outward from downtown Cincinnati. If you are driving a vehicle, whether it is a passenger car, bus (except trolley) or truck, give rides to as many people as can crowd in or on it.

Streets and roads will soon be marked to show the routes to be followed. These routes have been carefully planned as a result of over two years' study. **FOLLOW THEM.** If you live in Northern Kentucky, for your own sake and your family's sake, do not try to cross the bridges. You will be returned by other routes to your destination in due course of time. If you do try to cross, you would certainly be blocked by traffic at the southern end of the bridges, and you would only reduce your own chances, as well as the chances of many others.

If you are on foot and within a few blocks of a railroad yard, particularly the Union Terminal, or the yards along Millcreek, go to the yard and get on a train. **No ticket is necessary — Just get on**, no matter what kind of a train or car it is. The railroad company will run every locomotive and car they can move out of the danger area and there will be space for approximately 75,000 people. Once they are well out of the danger area, the train will be stopped near a reception center and you can then begin the reuniting process with any members of your family from whom you may have become separated.

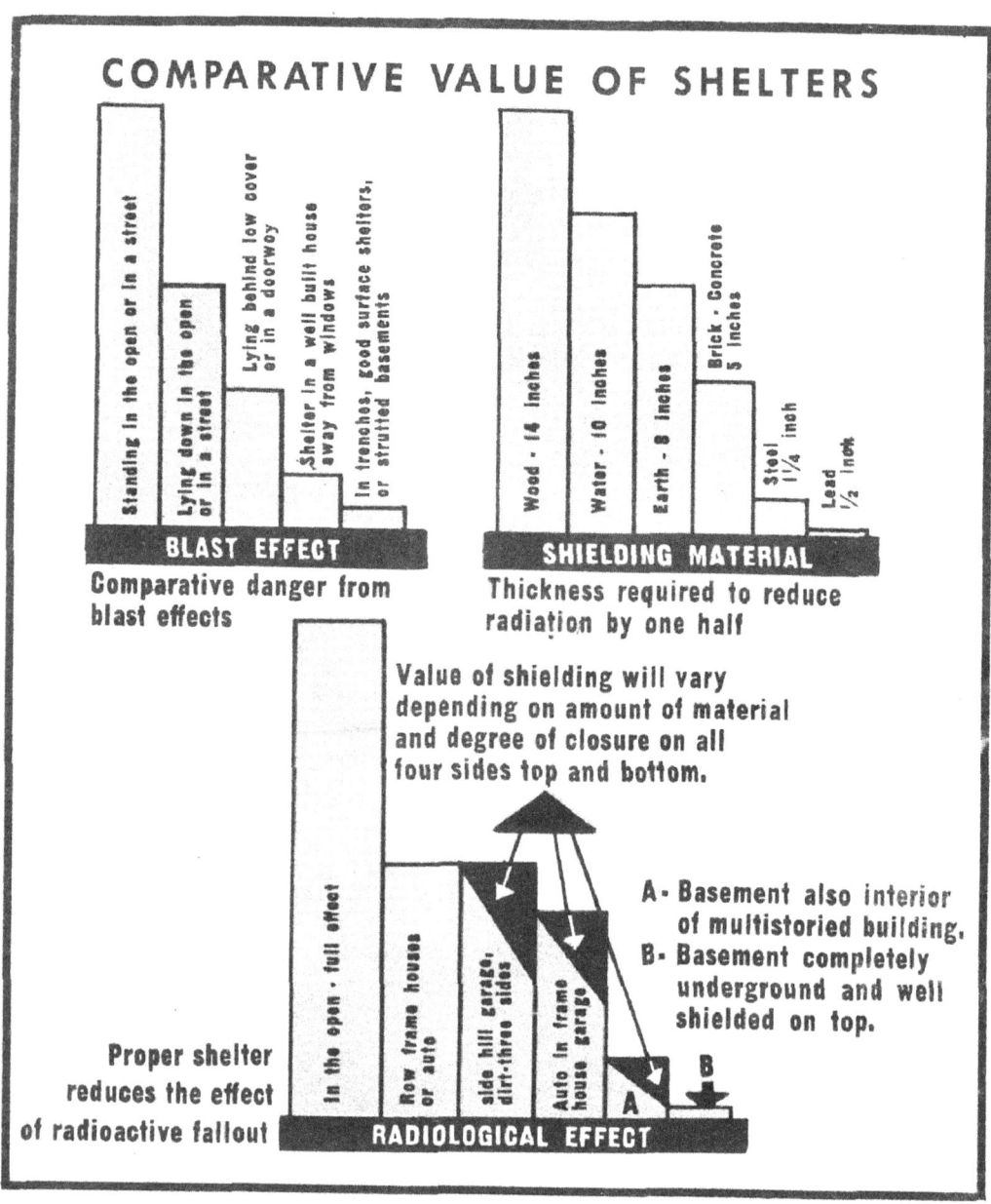

This chart described the value of shelters against the blast and radiation. Needless to say, being in a basement shelter was far more effective than being in the street (*Will to Survive*, Ohio Valley Defense Authority, 1955).

Survival of the Fittest

No city was safe. The United States, it was believed, could not stop an all-out Russian attack. And with the hydrogen bomb's dramatic increase in destructive power vs. the power of an atomic bomb, the best, and perhaps only, way to ensure survival was to get out of town — if you had time. Survival Is Up to You!, *published by the Portland (Oregon) Target Area Coordinating Council in 1960, provided an overview of the problem and instructions on how best to evacuate the city.*

The Problem

THE RUSSIANS HAVE A CAPABILITY OF ATTACKING ANY TARGET IN THE UNITED STATES. OUR MILITARY DEFENSES CANNOT BE EXPECTED TO PREVENT ALL WEAPONS FROM REACHING THEIR TARGETS IN AN ALL-OUT ATTACK ON THIS COUNTRY.

The Portland Target Area must be prepared for an attack involving one or more nuclear weapons as well as other forms of modern warfare. This could result in damage and destruction of relative minor significance up to complete and total destruction of the AIMING AREA with a change of radioactive contamination denying any permanent use of the large parts of the target area for many months or even years.

These are the facts that the citizens in this area *must* face.

Basic Policy

ALTHOUGH THERE ARE NO EASY SOLUTIONS FOR PROTECTION IN THIS ATOMIC AGE, THERE ARE DEFINITE DEFENSES WE CAN EMPLOY AGAINST NUCLEAR ATTACKS. ESSENTIALLY THESE ARE *EVACUATION* (PROTECTION BY MOVEMENT AWAY FROM THE TARGET AREA BEFORE AN ATTACK) AND *SHELTER* (PROTECTION FROM ATTACK WITHIN PROPERLY DESIGNED AND CONSTRUCTED FACILITIES).

Organized Planning

GOVERNMENTAL AGENCIES WORKING TOGETHER HAVE DEVELOPED A REALISTIC PLAN FOR THE EVACUATION OF THE PORTLAND TAR-

Survival Is Up to You!, Portland (Oregon) Target Area Coordinating Council, 1960.

GET AREA. THIS PLAN WILL WORK IF, AND *ONLY* IF, THE CITIZENS OF THIS AREA HAVE FAMILIARIZED THEMSELVES WITH THE PLAN AND HAVE A GENUINE DESIRE TO MAKE IT WORK.

The National Plan published by the Federal Office of Civil and Defense Mobilization established the framework within which all nonmilitary defense activities of the nation will function. Based upon the National Plan, each state develops its own Civil Defense Plan and the State Plan provides the basis for Civil Defense Plans of counties, cities, and towns, as required by Oregon State Law. However, it is equally important that school districts, businesses, commercial and manufacturing establishments, hospitals, and other institutions, as well as families and individuals plan for disaster operations. This latter planning is voluntary but is of equal importance with governmental planning if a realistic survival capability is to be developed.

HERE'S WHAT YOU MUST DO!

HERE'S WHAT YOU MUST DO *NOW* AS WELL AS THE *ACTION* YOU MUST TAKE WHEN THE WARNING SIGNALS SOUND.

General Preparations

1. *Family Planning*—MAKE SURE EVERY ADULT AND OLDER CHILD IN YOUR FAMILY HAS READ AND UNDERSTANDS THE INFORMATION IN THIS PAMPHLET. Call your family together for the purpose of discussing and preparing your family plan.

2. *Coordinated Family and School Plans*—IF YOU ARE A PARENT OF A SCHOOL CHILD, YOU WILL NEED TO COORDINATE YOUR FAMILY SURVIVAL PLAN FOR EVACUATION WITH THAT OF YOUR SCHOOL. You should contact your school authorities to learn whether your child will evacuate with other children directly from the school or will be sent home to evacuate with you or, if you are not at home, with a neighbor or family of a classmate. If your child evacuates directly from the school, you will want to know the means of transportation and planning destination for reception and care.

3. *Identification Tag*—In event of a major natural disaster or attack, many people may be temporarily confused and unable to think clearly—children may be separated from their families; other people may be badly hurt or dead. It is most important in disaster relief operations that parents be re-united with their children, families of the badly injured be notified of their condition and whereabouts, and the dead identified before burial. IN ORDER TO MAKE THE TASK OF IDENTIFICATION EASIER AND TO ALLEVIATE ANXIETY AS QUICKLY AS POSSIBLE, CIVIL DEFENSE AUTHORITIES STRONGLY URGE EVERYONE TO WEAR CONSTANTLY A METAL IDENTIFICATION TAG. Identification tags should include the wearer's full name, present address, birth date and indicate his religion. Blood type, if imprinted on the tag, should be confirmed by proper medical authorities. Names and addresses of companies that manufacture approved civil defense identification tags can be obtained from your civil defense office.

4. *Training for Emergencies*—THE MINIMUM TRAINING FOR EMERGENCIES SHOULD INCLUDE ONE PERSON IN EVERY FAMILY TRAINED IN *FIRST AID* PROCEDURES AND ONE PERSON IN *CARE OF SICK AND INJURED*. Additional training in other civil defense subjects for emergencies is available.

Part 7 — Evacuate

Evacuation Preparations

1. *Evacuation Signal* — MEMORIZE THE *EVACUATION SIGNAL* — 3 MINUTES *STEADY TONE* ON THE SIRENS OR HORNS — YOU MUST BE PREPARED TO EVACUATE IMMEDIATELY WHEN THIS SIGNAL SOUNDS.

2. *Transportation* — PLAN TO USE YOUR OWN CAR. IF YOU DON'T HAVE ONE, ARRANGE TO RIDE WITH A NEIGHBOR OR FELLOW EMPLOYEE. IN NEIGHBORHOODS WHERE ENOUGH CARS ARE NOT AVAILABLE IN THE DAYTIME, *CAR POOLS* SHOULD BE ARRANGED. Instead of one person taking the family car to work everyday, plans should be made for several persons to ride to work in one car, thus, leaving some cars at home for use in emergencies and for shopping and taking the children to school as well.

Your family car can be "four wheels to survival." Your car may be the means of saving your life. Keep it in good mechanical condition. *BE SURE YOU KEEP YOUR GAS TANK MORE THAN HALF FULL AT ALL TIMES SO YOU WILL ALWAYS HAVE A CAPABILITY TO EVACUATE IN AN EMERGENCY.*

3. Evacuation Kit — BASIC ITEMS FOR THE FAMILY EVACUATION KIT INCLUDE A THREE OR MORE DAYS SUPPLY OF FOOD AND WATER, FIRST AID ITEMS, FLASHLIGHT WITH EXTRA BATTERIES, EXTRA CLOTHING AND BLANKETS AS WELL AS A PORTABLE BATTERY RADIO IF THERE IS NO CAR RADIO. These items together with special medicines and any other specific needs should be packed and kept in the car at all times or ready to put in a car when the evacuation signal sounds.

4. *Evacuation Routes* — SPECIFIC EVACUATION ROUTES HAVE BEEN DESIGNATED TO ASSIST PEOPLE TO MOVE RAPIDLY USING ALL LANES FOR OUTBOUND MOVEMENT. It is important you study the evacuation route map and determine the route nearest your home, place of employment and any other location where you spend much time. Your family planning should not be considered complete until you have made a practice drive on your evacuation routes, particularly the one nearest your home. Follow the directions on the map and directions provided by the evacuation route signs posted along the routes. Your practice drive should be for a distance of at least 50 miles, both in the daytime and at night.

5. *Family Meeting Place* — The family meeting place should be a location outside the Portland Critical Target Area where members of the family can attempt to get together or send word of their condition and whereabouts following a major disaster. If possible, you should make arrangements *now* with relatives, friends or others for a suitable place where members of your family can stay. Do not select a place earmarked for other civil defense purposes.

Evacuation Action

Here's what you *must* or *must not* do when the evacuation signals sound —

1. Don't use your telephone.
2. Load your car with your evacuation kit, if it is not already there. If you don't have a car, check on your prearranged transportation.

3. Close blinds and windows and leave your home as you would if you were going away for a day or two.
4. If you have no transportation, start walking toward the nearest evacuation route where you can obtain a ride in a passing vehicle.
5. Do not go to your local school for your children unless you have previously agreed to participate in the school evacuation plan.
6. If you should be inbound, heading toward the city center, turn around and drive out and away from the city. Do not drive counter to the evacuation traffic pattern.
7. Keep your car windows open at least part way prior to an attack in order to equalize blast pressure. Following an attack and passage of the blast wave, car windows, doors and vents should be kept closed to prevent fallout material from entering.
8. Pick up pedestrians until your vehicle is full. Do not block traffic when you stop.
9. Move on the nearest evacuation route. Drive safely. In downtown Portland, follow the green traffic lights to get on an evacuation route. Do not cross or go counter to evacuation routes.
10. If cars are stalled or involved in an accident, assist in pushing them to one side and pick up their passengers.
11. Listen for information and instructions on your radio. *CONELRAD* broadcasts will be received at 640 or 1240 on your regular radio dial. If you don't hear any broadcasts at first, be patient until the *CONELRAD* broadcasting can begin.
12. Follow your evacuation route as indicated by the highway evacuation route signs or directions of traffic officers.
13. Do not stop at civil defense emergency aid areas unless it is impossible for you to go any further.
14. Follow directions of traffic officers. Do not stop or turn off until directed to do so.

Evacuation Rules and Routes

Follow the rules, know the signals, and, most important, follow the proper routes when evacuating the city. These were the life-saving points emphasized in the Nashville-Davidson County Civil Defense Survival Plan, *published in 1955.*

Air Raid Warning Signals

All citizens should familiarize themselves with the two types of warning signals which will be sounded by Civil Defense officials in times of emergency. They are:

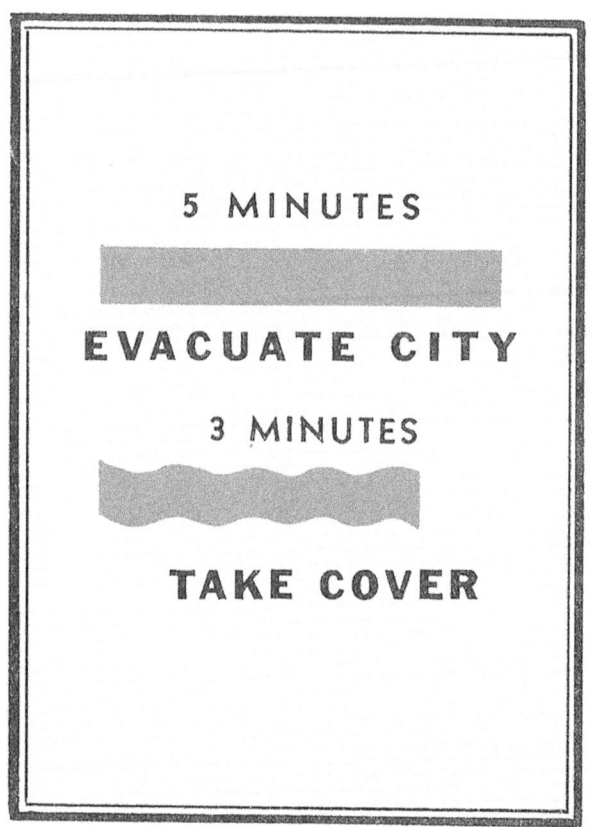

1. THE EVACUATION SIGNAL—a steady blast of five minutes' duration. The evacuation signal will indicate to the public, action to be taken (start evacuating the city). Civil Defense workers will go into action according to pre-arranged planning. Some will help speed the evacuation.

2. THE TAKE COVER SIGNAL—a wailing tone or series of short, up-and-down modulated blasts of three minutes' duration. The TAKE COVER signal will indicate that an attack is imminent and the public must take the best shelter immediately available. It will be assumed that insufficient time remains to begin or to complete an evacuation of the city.

More specific Civil Defense instructions will be given by all possible means of communication to supplement the evacuation and take cover signals. Means of communica-

Nashville-Davidson County Civil Defense Survival Plan, Nashville-Davidson County Civil Defense, 1955.

tions for this purpose will consist principally of radio, public address systems, and person-to-person contact by police and other officials.

Since hazard of radioactive fallout may preclude bringing the public out of shelters, the former "All Clear" signal has been eliminated according to the Federal Civil Defense officials. Instructions to come out of shelter areas will be given to the public by other means of communication.

Remember These Simple Rules ...

1. If the EVACUATION signal sounds, find the closest available transportation and begin evacuating the city.
2. If the TAKE COVER signal sounds and you are:
   AT HOME — Go to your basement, if you are close enough; or drop to the floor; get under a bed or heavy table.
   AT WORK — Drop to the floor; get under a desk or work bench.
   AT SCHOOL — Drop to the floor out of line of windows; bury face in arms.
   IN THE OPEN — Drop to the ground or dive for any sort of cover; bury face in arms.
   IN VEHICLES — Drop to the floor; bury face in arms.

Here Is What You Do ...

As soon as you hear the Evacuation Signal on the sirens, START MOVING OUT! Or, if you are out where there are no sirens (parts of Davidson County) and you first hear about the emergency over the radio or TV, START MOVING OUT! Stay calm, but START MOVING! Of course, we cannot all move out right away. But if each of us knows what to do and follows directions, we can all move with less trouble and more speed. Your house, if it survives bombing, and its contents will be policed by local police authorities until you return.

Get Beyond the Safety Line ...

Wherever you are, when you hear the Evacuation Signal, get out of the danger zone the best way you can. Use your own car if you have one and can get to it. Or, hitch a ride with others in any transportation available. In a crisis like this, the automobile may be your best friend, so keep it in good repair and half full of gasoline at all times. If you have no car or transportation, then start walking.

Evacuation Instructions

1. **WHEN YOU HEAR THE EVACUATION SIGNAL:**
   Keep calm — DO NOT USE THE TELEPHONE. Immediately, turn your radio to 640 or 1240 on your dial. Listen for further instructions while you are preparing yourself and family for immediate evacuation. Get your emergency evacuation kit, which should include food, water, first-aid kit, extra clothing, a battery radio, and may

include blankets, flashlight, money. You should have it packed, ready to go, but if you have not, collect it quickly and place in the car. Check on the gas tank of your car (remember, try to keep it at least half full at all times. It will be too late to purchase gas once the signals have sounded).

2. **EVACUATION ROUTES (OR ESCAPE WAYS):**
Study maps ... which show the evacuation routes or escape ways for Nashville and Davidson County. Become familiar with ... your destination and reception points. Choose NOW the nearest and the most accessible one for you and your family by vehicle or on foot; when at home, when at work, when shopping, when at play, when at church. WHEREVER YOU AND EACH MEMBER OF YOUR FAMILY MAY BE, if and when the evacuation signal sounds. All Evacuation Routes will be ONE-WAY OUTBOUND ONLY. Do not try to cross any of them. Obey instructions of police and authorized Civil Defense personnel, for the safety of all.

3. **HOW TO GET OUT OF THE DOWNTOWN AREA:**
    A. Moving vehicles:
    All traffic flow with normal traffic regulations, observing signals, within the boundaries of the "Get-A-Way" area. When moving to the streets marked in heavy red [on your evacuation map], be extremely cautious, especially at intersections. This area is designed to allow you to evacuate in the general direction of your home or family. Once out of the Get-A-Way area, all traffic will be one way OUTWARD.
    B. Curb-parked vehicles:
    Get to your vehicle quickly and proceed as for moving vehicles.
    C. Vehicles in parking lots or on the ground level of parking buildings:
    Go quickly to your vehicle at the parking lot. Drive from there to the nearest most accessible evacuation route and move outward.
    D. Vehicles in parking buildings:
    Except for vehicles parked on the ground level, it will probably be impractical to move any vehicles from multi-storied parking buildings. Drivers and passengers of such vehicles should take action as for pedestrians.
    E. Pedestrians:
    If not already on one, go to the nearest street marked in red ... and continue outward until you are offered a ride in a private, commercial, or public vehicle. Note also railroad and bus instructions.

4. **LOAD YOUR VEHICLE WITH PASSENGERS:**
While moving to an evacuation route or while traveling thereon, load your vehicle to capacity. Many people will be on foot. However, be sure that such loading does not impede the flow of evacuation traffic. Keep on the outside lanes until your vehicle is filled. Fully loaded vehicles use center lanes.

5. **DOUBLING UP TRANSPORTATION WITH YOUR NEIGHBORS:**
Transportation for your family should be given first consideration. If you are a one-car family, double up with some neighbor who works at, or on the route to, or in the vicinity of, your place of business or employment. Then, you and your neighbor, alternate each week driving to and from work. The auto that stays home would be

available to carry the two families to safety. The wife with the car will be able to collect the other family and its Survival Kit and get out of the target area on a predetermined route. Families doubling up their transportation should agree to keep the car in good operating order and at no time have less than a HALF TANK OF FUEL. Tire chains, spare tire, and tools should be permanently stored in each vehicle.

6. **GETTING YOUR FAMILY TOGETHER AGAIN:**
Families should plan NOW how to get back together again. A good plan is to pick a family meeting place (such as the home of a friend or relative) at least 30 to 40 miles from Nashville. Then after each member of the family gets out of the danger area, he can try to get to the meeting place or at least to get word there, about himself. This way, it should not take long to get the family together again.

7. **RAILROAD LOADING AREAS:**
If you are in the vicinity of ... loading areas with no car, or a ride, or your parked car is too distant or is in a multi-storied parking building, go to the nearest railway loading area as quickly as possible and board a railway car.

8. **PUBLIC TRANSPORTATION:**
Outbound buses and those at terminals or garages should load to capacity while proceeding to the nearest, most accessible, evacuation route and keep moving outward. Inbound buses should turn onto a side street; load to capacity while proceeding to nearest, most accessible, evacuation route and move outward. Some buses will be reserved to assist in evacuation of schools, hospitals, and institutions. The action to be taken by each bus driver and to be announced by him to the passengers will be directed by the Nashville Transit Company, or other officials.

9. **SCHOOL EVACUATION:**
Schools will be evacuated according to prearranged plans. Do not attempt to pick your child up at school, unless you have agreed to assist in the school evacuation program. Your child will be taken care of and evacuated by the school authorities under civil defense directions.

Your Decision ...

Although there is no easy solution to the nuclear age, Civil Defense gives you a defense against H-bombs, the best being distance and shelter. But it is YOUR decision. Survival depends mainly on individual judgment and action.

Stay calm, be patient, obey instructions. With everyone's cooperation, all can move with less trouble and more speed. In some safe areas, traffic authorities might direct you into side roads or to temporary parking lots off the highway in order to speed movement of traffic farther back. **Obey authorities promptly.**

THE ONE CARDINAL RULE — Take care of your own problem of getting out of the city. Instruct members of your family to do likewise. Don't waste even a few seconds trying to contact members of your family. You will not be able to. Of most comfort to each individual would be a thorough, advance understanding in your family that all will follow evacuation instructions, and then meet at some point far from the city later.

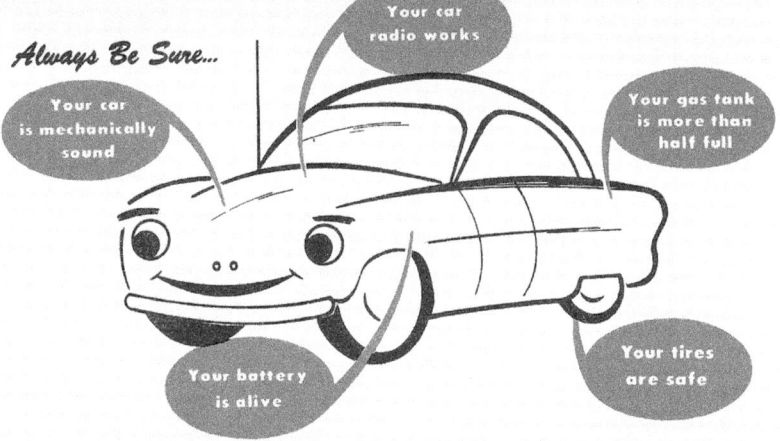

4 WHEELS TO SURVIVAL

Always Be Sure...

- Your car is mechanically sound
- Your car radio works
- Your gas tank is more than half full
- Your battery is alive
- Your tires are safe

Your Family Car—*The Difference between Life and Death?*

You may think your family car is indispensable under ordinary conditions—but how much more important it becomes in an emergency. Here are some of the bonuses a well-cared-for automobile can give you:

SHELTER

Automobiles provide a degree of protection against blast, as well as radioactive fallout. Remember, though—LOWER your windows before an attack to equalize pressures and prevent glass breakage, and RAISE your windows after an attack to keep out dust and debris (which may be radioactive).

INFORMATION

If your car radio dial is not already marked, mark the 640 and 1240 Conelrad frequencies, for they will be your source of information and instruction under attack conditions.

FOOD

Your emergency food kit with your 7-day food supply should be kept in a carton, ready to put in the trunk of your family car. Everything to make your family self-sufficient for several days, if necessary, should be included. Your car can be a portable house.

MOBILITY

Pre-attack evacuation, as well as many other civil defense activities, depends upon your ability to move away from approaching danger. Learn how to conserve gasoline—you may not be able to buy any. And keep on hand good maps of your city and the surrounding area.

LAST BUT NOT LEAST . . . the rules of safe driving and courtesy to others become doubly important in an emergency. REMEMBER

DO . . .
Obey police and civil defense authorities.
If you have room, pick up pedestrians.
If your car stalls, get it off the road.

DON'T . . .
Crowd or try to beat the other fellow.
Be impatient or lean on the horn—you may panic others.

Automobiles had a special importance during the 1950s. As this illustration states so clearly, the family car represented "the difference between life and death." The car was a bomb shelter, a storage device for food, and transportation for a quick evacuation from the city. (*Nashville-Davidson County Civil Defense Survival Plan*, Nashville-Davidson County Civil Defense, 1955)

Don't Be There

The Birmingham-Jefferson County (Alabama) Civil Defense Corps published the most explicit title of the 1950s: When the Bomb Goes Off— Don't Be There! *The brochure outlined the emergency evacuation plan in the event the Soviet Union launched a successful H-bomb attack.*

The following plan is submitted for your information and guidance in the event of an enemy attack on the Birmingham area.

1. IT CAN HAPPEN HERE ...

Our detection system, fighter planes, anti-aircraft guns, and guided missiles are all being made bigger and better. But still, one enemy plane getting through with a modern H-Bomb could destroy or severely damage more than half the Birmingham area.

2. YOU CAN STILL SURVIVE ...

Because of this powerful weapon, a new Civil Defense plan has been made. Downtown Birmingham probably would be the most likely target due to its heavy population. However, the Fairfield-Ensley industrial area and Bessemer are also prime targets and in all probability would be bombed. When a bomb drops, the further you are from the danger zone, the best your chances of survival.

3. YOU HAVE TIME ...

Living in the southern part of the United States, we can be fairly sure of a two- to four-hour WARNING before the enemy could get here. Even this amount of time may not be enough for everyone to get far enough away to save himself. But one thing is sure! The farther away we get, the better our chances. Later on, as our continental warning system is improved, we may get 4 to 6 hours ... enough time for almost all of us to get out of the danger zone.

4. CIVIL DEFENSE ACTION SIGNALS ...

Every person should be trained to act instantly when a public action signal sounds. Every person should know the official civil defense instructions for taking action if an attack is threatened.

The members of your family or your business organization may have only a limited time to take protective measures if an attack should come. That is why it is important to plan what to do ahead of time and to practice doing it. Whether there is sufficient warning time to evacuate our city or only time to take shelter in our homes or places of business, chances of survival will be better if you know what to do and are trained to act.

There will be two (2) Civil Defense public action signals sounded on Air Raid Warning Sirens:

1. The Alert-Evacuation Signal,
2. The Take Cover Signal.

THE ALERT EVACUATION SIGNAL: A steady blast of 3 to 5 minutes duration on Air Raid sirens means that enemy planes are heading our way and that an attack on our city is probable and will be the signal for evacuation and for the mobilization of our Civil Defense forces. Signals to be repeated 2 or more times.

TAKE COVER SIGNAL: A wailing tone on Air Raid sirens or a series of short blasts of 3-minutes duration means that attack is imminent and that you must take the best available shelter immediately. Signals to be repeated 2 or more times.

The said "Evacuation" and "Take Cover" signals will be the same in all cities throughout the United States. If you should be in some other city and hear them, you will know their meaning.

5. EVACUATION SIGNALS — HERE'S WHAT TO DO ...

As soon as you hear the Alert-Evacuation signal on the Air Raid sirens, immediately turn your radio to 640 or 1240 on your dial. (This is usually found at 64 or 124 on most radio dials.) All radio and TV stations will go off the air on receipt of the Warning Yellow from the Air Force, but all AM stations will immediately return on the CONELRAD (Controlled Electronic Radio) frequency, which is located at 640 or 1240 on your dial. Listen for further instructions while you are preparing yourself and family for immediate evacuation. START MOVING OUT. Stay calm, but START MOVING! If each of us knows what to do and follows directions, we can all move with less trouble and more speed.

6. MOVE OUT — NEVER ACROSS ...

Study the ... planned escape routes. CHOOSE NOW those that are best for you and your family. PLAN how you can best reach them. When the EVACUATION SIGNAL sounds, all escape routes will be one way — OUTBOUND ONLY! Do not try to cross any of these escape routes. Police will stop you. Besides, traffic going outward will be so heavy that you cannot cross. Head in one direction only — OUTBOUND — the way traffic is moving. You may have to be patient but stay calm, wait, and your turn will come to get on the escape routes.

WHEN THE BOMB GOES OFF
—don't BE there!

BIRMINGHAM
AND
JEFFERSON COUNTY
CIVIL DEFENSE

COL. U. N. JAMES (Retd)
Coordinator-Director

FERD F. WEIL
Chief, Downtown Evacuation

JAMES W. MORGAN   CHAS. E. HARRISON
(Mayor, Birmingham)   *(County Commissioner)*
General Chairman   *Co-General Chairman*

Printed by Alabama Power Company for Birmingham-Jefferson County (Ala.) Civil Defense Corps as a public service.

When the Bomb Goes Off— Don't Be There!, Birmingham-Jefferson County (Alabama) Civil Defense Corps, 1955.

7. WHAT ABOUT SCHOOLS, HOSPITALS, ETC. ...?

A special plan for evacuating school children has been worked out with school authorities and all those concerned are fully informed.

A study and plan for evacuation of hospitals is being made by medical authorities and Civilian Defense Headquarters.

8. GET OUT TO SAFETY ...

Wherever you are, when you hear the Evacuation Signal on your Air Raid sirens, get out of the danger area the best way that you can. Use your own car if you can get to it. If not, go to your nearest automobile dealer who will furnish you with transportation. If you are in the downtown area, in addition to automobile dealers, you may obtain transportation at the following places:

- Terminal Station
- L&N Railroad Station
- Greyhound Bus Terminal
- Greyhound Bus Garage

If you wish, you may hitch a ride with others in any transportation available. In a crisis like this, the automobile will be your best friend. EVERY CAR SHOULD BE FULL. If you cannot find a ride, start walking, as organized public transportation may be able to pick you up enroute. Get as far away from downtown Birmingham as possible—up to forty (40) miles or more if you can. You may be delayed on the way out more than once, but STAY WITH YOUR RIDE, if you have one. Thus, you will still get out faster and farther than by walking. If the car in front of you breaks down or runs out of gasoline, help push it off of the highway and distribute its passengers in other cars. Do not permit delays because of disabled automobiles.

9. SUBURBAN AREAS ...

If you live in the areas immediately outside Birmingham—such as Tarrant, Mountain Brook, Homewood, Fairfield and Bessemer—there are many county and secondary roads that may be used to get you to safety. Select the one *NOW* that is best suited for evacuation of your family.

10. IF YOU ARE ALREADY 8 MILES OR MORE FROM DOWNTOWN ...

You can probably live through an H-Bomb attack where you are if you get into a good shelter such as the basement of a substantial building, a cyclone shelter, or a well-built bomb shelter. BUT YOU CAN INCREASE YOUR CHANCES OF SURVIVAL BY MOVING STILL FARTHER OUT!

11. WHAT ABOUT "FALL-OUT"?

Radioactive material deposited during "fall-out" may or may not be visible.

Some of the radioactive particles will spill out in the immediate area of the explosion, but others may be carried by the upper winds for many miles. Sooner or later they settle to earth. This is called "fall-out." Normal amounts of radiation are harmless. It is only when it is present in large amounts, such as are created by ground burst of hydrogen or the larger atomic bombs, that radioactive "fall-out" can cause serious injury or death to those without protective cover.

The danger from radioactive "fall-out" will begin about 1½ hours after the bomb explodes. The basement of a building, which is several stories high, is the safest place for your protection from this "fall-out," but any type of cover reduces the danger. The hazard or amounts of exposure from "fall-out," on the first floor inside of an ordinary frame house, would be about one-half of what it would be outside of the house. Even more safety or protection could be expected if you are inside a brick or stone house. Taking shelter in the basement of an average house would reduce the danger to about one-tenth of what it would be out of doors. Shelter in an old-fashioned cyclone cellar, with a covering of earth three (3) feet thick, would give you almost complete safety.

The more solid material you can get between you and the "fall-out," the safer you will be.

12. FOOD, WATER, CLOTHING ...

At assembly areas in nearby cities and towns, beyond the danger zone, arrangements will be made to feed, clothe, and shelter thousands who will need help. The State Civil Defense Agency, this Headquarters, and our mutual-aid counties are working out plans to accomplish this. But you will be better able to survive if you can take care of yourself for awhile. Plan to take with you your own food, water, and clothing.

13. GETTING YOUR FAMILY TOGETHER AGAIN ...

Families should plan now how to get back together again. A good plan is to pick a family meeting place (such as the home of a friend or relative) 15 to 50 miles from Birmingham. Then, after each member of the family gets out of the danger area, he can try to get to this meeting place or at least to get word to it about himself. In this way, it should not take too long to reassemble the family.

14. TAKE COVER SIGNAL ...

"TAKE-COVER" is a three-minute wailing sound on the Air Raid sirens or short blasts on any whistles repeated several times. It means that attack is very close. When you hear this signal, GET INTO THE BEST SHELTER YOU CAN FIND IMMEDIATELY! If in a car and no better shelter is near, crunch down in the car. Keep your radio turned to 640 or 1240 on the dial for further information and instructions. Open car windows.

15. AIR RAID TEST ALERTS ...

Air Raid sirens will be tested every Wednesday at 11:00 A.M. The purpose of these tests are to keep you familiar with the signals and also to see that all equipment is in good working condition. During the said tests, the "Evacuation" and "Take Cover" signals will be sounded for only one period of three minutes each.

16. THE DOWNTOWN GETAWAY AREA ...

Permits traffic to move outward in any direction; all drivers must observe traffic signals and one-way streets. OUTSIDE OF THE DOWNTOWN AREA — All traffic will move in one direction only — *Outbound*, and will disregard the traffic light signals. Traffic on these escape highways will be controlled by Police, Military, and Civil Defense personnel.

Part 8

Peace ... or Else

It Could Happen Here!, Veterans of Foreign Wars Post No. 3477, Athens, Ohio, no date.

"Atoms for Peace"

By 1953, both the United States and the Soviet Union had exploded hydrogen bombs, greatly escalating the Cold War. Realizing the inherent dangers facing the U.S.—and the world— President Dwight D. Eisenhower addressed the United Nations on December 8 of that year in a speech titled "Atoms for Peace," which would later become a program that supplied equipment and information to schools, hospitals, and other institutions within the country and throughout the world.

Madam President and Members of the General Assembly:

When Secretary General Hammarskjold's invitation to address this General Assembly reached me in Bermuda, I was just beginning a series of conferences with the Prime Ministers and Foreign Ministers of Great Britain and of France. Our subject was some of the problems that beset our world.

During the remainder of the Bermuda Conference, I had constantly in mind that ahead of me lay a great honor. That honor is mine today, as I stand here, privileged to address the General Assembly of the United Nations.

At the same time that I appreciate the distinction of addressing you, I have a sense of exhilaration as I look upon this Assembly. Never before in history has so much hope for so many people been gathered together in a single organization. Your deliberations and decisions during these somber years have already realized part of those hopes.

But the great tests and the great accomplishments still lie ahead. And in the confident expectation of those accomplishments, I would use the office which, for the time being, I hold, to assure you that the Government of the United States will remain steadfast in its support of this body. This we shall do in the conviction that you will provide a great share of the wisdom, of the courage, and the faith which can bring to this world lasting peace for all nations, and happiness and well-being for all men.

Clearly, it would not be fitting for me to take this occasion to present to you a unilateral American report on Bermuda. Nevertheless, I assure you that in our deliberations on that lovely island, we sought to invoke those same great concepts of universal peace and human dignity which are so cleanly etched in your Charter. Neither would it be a measure of this great opportunity merely to recite, however hopefully, pious platitudes.

I therefore decided that this occasion warranted my saying to you some of the things that have been on the minds and hearts of my legislative and executive associates, and on mine, for a great many months — thoughts I had originally planned to say primarily to the American people.

President Dwight D. Eisenhower, concerned over the rapid escalation of nuclear weapons, addressed the United Nations on December 8, 1953, on the need to work toward peace. His speech, titled "Atoms for Peace," set the stage for an international program that helped schools, hospitals, and other institutions. Unfortunately, his efforts did not lessen the tensions of the Cold War (Dwight D. Eisenhower Presidential Library & Museum).

I know that the American people share my deep belief that if a danger exists in the world, it is a danger shared by all; and equally, that if hope exists in the mind of one nation, that hope should be shared by all.

Finally, if there is to be advanced any proposal designed to ease even by the smallest measure the tensions of today's world, what more appropriate audience could there be than the members of the General Assembly of the United Nations. I feel impelled to speak today in a language that in a sense is new, one which I, who have spent so much of my life in the military profession, would have preferred never to use. That new language is the language of atomic warfare.

The atomic age has moved forward at such a pace that every citizen of the world should have some comprehension, at least in comparative terms, of the extent of this development, of the utmost significance to every one of us. Clearly, if the peoples of the world are to conduct an intelligent search for peace, they must be armed with the significant facts of today's existence.

My recital of atomic danger and power is necessarily stated in United States terms, for these are the only incontrovertible facts that I know. I need hardly point out to this Assembly, however, that this subject is global, not merely national in character.

On July 16, 1945, the United States set off the world's first atomic explosion.

Since that date in 1945, the United States of America has conducted forty-two test explosions. Atomic bombs today are more than twenty-five times as powerful as the weapons with which the atomic age dawned, while hydrogen weapons are in the ranges of millions of tons of TNT equivalent.

Today, the United States stockpile of atomic weapons, which, of course, increases daily, exceeds by many times the total [explosive] equivalent of the total of all bombs and all shells that came from every plane and every gun in every theatre of war in all the years of World War II.

A single air group, whether afloat or land based, can now deliver to any reachable target a destructive cargo exceeding in power all the bombs that fell on Britain in all of World War II. In size and variety, the development of atomic weapons has been no less remarkable. The development has been such that atomic weapons have virtually achieved conventional status within our armed services.

In the United States, the Army, the Navy, the Air Force, and the Marine Corps are all capable of putting this weapon to military use. But the dread secret and the fearful engines of atomic might are not ours alone.

In the first place, the secret is possessed by our friends and allies, Great Britain and Canada, whose scientific genius made a tremendous contribution to our original discoveries and the designs of atomic bombs.

The secret is also known by the Soviet Union.

The Soviet Union has informed us that, over recent years, it has devoted extensive resources to atomic weapons. During this period the Soviet Union has exploded a series of atomic devices, including at least one involving thermo-nuclear reactions. If at one time the Unites States possessed what might have been called a monopoly of atomic power, that monopoly ceased to exist several years ago.

Therefore, although our earlier start has permitted us to accumulate what is today a great quantitative advantage, the atomic realities of today comprehend two facts of even greater significance.

First, the knowledge now possessed by several nations will eventually be shared by others, possibly all others.

Second, even a vast superiority in numbers of weapons, and a consequent capability of devastating retaliation, is no preventive, of itself, against the fearful material damage and toll of human lives that would be inflicted by surprise aggression. The free world, at least dimly aware of these facts, has naturally embarked on a large program of warning and defense systems. That program will be accelerated and expanded. But let no one think that the expenditure of vast sums for weapons and systems of defense can guarantee absolute safety for the cities and citizens of any nation. The awful arithmetic of the atomic bomb does not permit of any such easy solution. Even against the most powerful defense, an aggressor in possession of the effective minimum number of atomic bombs for a surprise attack could probably place a sufficient number of his bombs on the chosen targets to cause hideous damage.

Should such an atomic attack be launched against the United States, our reactions would be swift and resolute. But for me to say that the defense capabilities of the United States are such that they could inflict terrible losses upon an aggressor, for me to say that the retaliation capabilities of the Unites States are so great that such an aggressor's land would be laid waste, all this, while fact, is not the true expression of the purpose and the hope of the United States.

To pause there would be to confirm the hopeless finality of a belief that two atomic colossi are doomed malevolently to eye each other indefinitely across a trembling world. To stop there would be to accept hope — helplessly the probability of civilization destroyed, the annihilation of the irreplaceable heritage of mankind handed down to use generation from generation, and the condemnation of mankind to begin all over again the age-old struggle upward from savagery toward decency, and right, and justice. Surely no sane member of the human race could discover victory in such desolation.

Could anyone wish his name to be coupled by history with such human degradation and destruction? Occasional pages of history do record the faces of the "great destroyers," but the whole book of history reveals mankind's never-ending quest for peace and mankind's God-given capacity to build.

It is with the book of history, and not with isolated pages, that the United States will ever wish to be identified. My country wants to be constructive, not destructive. It wants agreements, not wars, among nations. It wants itself to live in freedom and in the confidence that the people of every other nation enjoy equally the right of choosing their own way of life.

So my country's purpose is to help us move out of the dark chamber of horrors into the light, to find a way by which the minds of men, the hopes of men, the souls of men everywhere, can move forward toward peace and happiness and well-being.

In this quest, I know that we must not lack patience. I know that in a world divided, such as ours today, salvation cannot be attained by one dramatic act. I know that many steps will have to be taken over many months before the world can look at itself one day and truly realize that a new climate of mutually peaceful confidence is abroad in the world. But I know, above all else, that we must start to take these steps now.

The United States and its allies, Great Britain and France, have, over the past months, tried to take some of these steps. Let no one say that we shun the conference table. On the record has long stood the request of the United States, Great Britain, and France to negotiate with the Soviet Union the problems of a divided Germany. On that record has long stood the request of the same three nations to negotiate an Austrian peace treaty. On the same record still stands the request of the United Nations to negotiate the problems of Korea.

Most recently we have received from the Soviet Union what is in effect an expression of willingness to hold a four-Power meeting. Along with our allies, Great Britain and France, we were pleased to see that his note did not contain the unacceptable preconditions previously put forward. As you already know from our joint Bermuda communiqué, the United States, Great Britain, and France have agreed promptly to meet with the Soviet Union.

The Government of the United States approaches this conference with hopeful sincerity. We will bend every effort of our minds to the single purpose of emerging from that conference with tangible results towards peace, the only true way of lessening international tension. We never have, we never will, propose or suggest that the Soviet Union surrender what is rightfully theirs. We will never say that the people of Russia are an enemy with whom we have no desire ever to deal or mingle in friendly and fruitful relationship.

On the contrary, we hope that this coming conference may initiate a relationship with the Soviet Union which will eventually bring about a free intermingling of the peoples of the East and of the West—the one sure, human way of developing the understanding required for confident and peaceful relations.

Instead of the discontent which is now settling upon Eastern Germany, occupied Austria, and the countries of Eastern Europe, we seek a harmonious family of free European nations, with none a threat to the other, and least of all a threat to the peoples of Russia. Beyond the turmoil and strife and misery of Asia, we seek peaceful opportunity for these peoples to develop their natural resources and to elevate their lives.

These are not idle words or shallow visions. Behind them lies a story of nations lately come to independence, not as a result of war, but through free grant or peaceful negotiation. There is a record already written of assistance gladly given by nations of the West to needy peoples and to those suffering the temporary effects of famine, drought, and natural disaster. These are deeds of peace. They speak more loudly than promises or protestations of peaceful intent. But I do not wish to rest either upon the reiteration of past proposals or the restatement of past deeds. The gravity of the time is such that every new avenue of peace, no matter how dimly discernible, should be explored. There is at least one new avenue of peace which has not yet been well explored—an avenue now laid out by the General Assembly of the Unites Nations.

In its resolution of November 18th, 1953, this General Assembly suggested—and I quote—"that the Disarmament Commission study the desirability of establishing a sub-committee consisting of representatives of the Powers principally involved, which should seek in private an acceptable solution and report such a solution to the General Assembly and to the Security Council not later than September 1, of 1954."

The United States, heeding the suggestion of the General Assembly of the United Nations, is instantly prepared to meet privately with such other countries as may be "principally involved," to seek "an acceptable solution" to the atomic armaments race which overshadows not only the peace, but the very life of the world. We shall carry into these private or diplomatic talks a new conception.

The United States would seek more than the mere reduction or elimination of atomic materials for military purposes. It is not enough to take this weapon out of the hands of the soldiers. It must be put into the hands of those who will know how to strip its military casing and adapt it to the arts of peace.

The United States knows that if the fearful trend of atomic military build-up can be reversed, this greatest of destructive forces can be developed into a great boon, for the benefit of all mankind. The United States knows that peaceful power from atomic energy is no dream of the future. That capability, already proved, is here, now, today. Who can doubt, if the entire body of the world's scientists and engineers had adequate amounts of fissionable material with which to test and develop their ideas, that this capability would rapidly be transformed into universal, efficient, and economic usage?

To hasten the day when fear of the atom will begin to disappear from the minds of people and the governments of the East and West, there are certain steps that can be taken now. I therefore make the following proposals:

The governments principally involved, to the extent permitted by elementary prudence, to begin now and continue to make joint contributions from their stockpiles of normal uranium and fissionable materials to an international atomic energy agency. We would expect that such an agency would be set up under the aegis of the United Nations.

The ratios of contributions, the procedures, and other details would properly be within the scope of the "private conversations" I have referred to earlier.

The United States is prepared to undertake these explorations in good faith. Any partner of the United States acting in the same good faith will find the United States a not unreasonable or ungenerous associate.

Undoubtedly, initial and early contributions to this plan would be small in quantity. However, the proposal has the great virtue that it can be undertaken without the irritations and mutual suspicions incident to any attempt to set up a completely acceptable system of world-wide inspection and control.

The atomic energy agency could be made responsible for the impounding, storage, and protection of the contributed fissionable and other materials. The ingenuity of our scientists will provide special, safe conditions under which such a bank of fissionable material can be made essentially immune to surprise seizure.

The more important responsibility of this atomic energy agency would be to devise methods whereby this fissionable material would be allocated to serve the peaceful pursuits of mankind. Experts would be mobilized to apply atomic energy to the needs of agriculture, medicine, and other peaceful activities. A special purpose would be to provide abundant electrical energy in the power-starved areas of the world. Thus the contributing Powers would be dedicating some of their strength to serve the needs rather than the fears of mankind.

The United States would be more than willing—it would be proud to take up with others "principally involved" the development of plans whereby such peaceful use of atomic energy would be expedited.

Of those "principally involved" the Soviet Union must, of course, be one. I would be prepared to submit to the Congress of the United States, and with every expectation of approval, any such plan that would, first, encourage world-wide investigation into the most effective peacetime uses of fissionable material, and with the certainty that they [the investigators] had all the material needed for the conduct of all experiments that were appropriate; second, begin to diminish the potential destructive power of the world's atomic stockpiles; third, allow all peoples of all nations to see that, in this enlightened age, the great Powers of the earth, both of the East and of the West, are interested in human aspirations first rather than in building up the armaments of war; fourth, open up a new channel for peaceful discussion and initiate at least a new approach to the many difficult problems that must be solved in both private and public conversations, if the world is to shake off the inertia imposed by fear and is to make positive progress toward peace.

Against the dark background of the atomic bomb, the United States does not wish merely to present strength, but also the desire and the hope for peace.

The coming months will be fraught with fateful decisions. In this Assembly, in the capitals and military headquarters of the world, in the hearts of men everywhere, be they governed or governors, may they be the decisions which will lead this world out of fear and into peace.

To the making of these fateful decisions, the United States pledges before you, and therefore before the world, its determination to help solve the fearful atomic dilemma — to devote its entire heart and mind to find the way by which the miraculous inventiveness of man shall not be dedicated to his death, but consecrated to his life.

I again thank the delegates for the great honor they have done me in inviting me to appear before them and in listening me — to me so courteously. Thank you.

Nuclear Test Ban Treaty

As the United States and Soviet Union increased their war readiness, and China moved ever closer to testing its first atomic bomb (exploded on October 16, 1964), President John F. Kennedy went on radio and television to address the American people on July 26, 1963, to urge support for a ban on nuclear tests in the atmosphere, underwater, and in outer space — which later became the Partial Test Ban Treaty.

Good evening, my fellow citizens:

I speak to you tonight in a spirit of hope. Eighteen years ago, the advent of nuclear weapons changed the course of the world as well as the war. Since that time, all mankind has been struggling to escape from the darkening prospect of mass destruction on earth. In an age when both sides have come to possess enough nuclear power to destroy the human race several times over, the world of communism and the world of free choice have been caught up in a vicious circle of conflicting ideology and interest. Each increase of tension has produced an increase of arms; each increase of arms has produced an increase of tension.

In these years, the United States and the Soviet Union have frequently communicated suspicion and warnings to each other, but very rarely hope. Our representatives have met at the summit and at the brink; they have met in Washington and in Moscow; in Geneva and at the United Nations. But too often these meetings have produced only darkness, discord, or disillusion.

Yesterday a shaft of light cut into the darkness. Negotiations were concluded in Moscow on a treaty to ban all nuclear tests in the atmosphere, in outer space, and under water. For the first time, an agreement has been reached on bringing the forces of nuclear destruction under international control — a goal first sought in 1946 when Bernard Baruch presented a comprehensive control plan to the United Nations.

That plan, and many subsequent disarmament plans, large and small, have all been blocked by those opposed to international inspection. A ban on nuclear tests, however, requires on-the-spot inspection only for underground tests. This Nation now possesses a variety of techniques to detect the nuclear tests of other nations which are conducted in the air or under water, for such tests produce unmistakable signs which our modern instruments can pick up.

The treaty initialed yesterday, therefore, is a limited treaty which permits continued underground testing and prohibits only those tests that we ourselves can police. It requires no control posts, no onsite inspection, no international body.

President Kennedy delivers a radio and television address on the Partial Test Ban Treaty on July 26, 1963, from the Oval Office in the White House (photograph by Abbie Rowe, National Park Service, in the John F. Kennedy Presidential Library and Museum, Boston).

We should also understand that it has other limits as well. Any nation which signs the treaty will have an opportunity to withdraw if it finds that extraordinary events related to the subject matter of the treaty have jeopardized its supreme interests; and no nation's right of self-defense will in any way be impaired. Nor does this treaty mean an end to the threat of nuclear war. It will not reduce nuclear stockpiles; it will not halt the production of nuclear weapons; it will not restrict their use in time of war.

Nevertheless, this limited treaty will radically reduce the nuclear testing which would otherwise be conducted on both sides; it will prohibit the United States, the United Kingdom, the Soviet Union, and all others who sign it, from engaging in the atmospheric tests which have so alarmed mankind; and it offers to all the world a welcome sign of hope.

For this is not a unilateral moratorium, but a specific and solemn legal obligation. While it will not prevent this Nation from testing underground, or from being ready to conduct atmospheric tests if the acts of others so require, it gives us a concrete opportunity to extend its coverage to other nations and later to other forms of nuclear tests.

This treaty is in part the product of Western patience and vigilance. We have made clear—most recently in Berlin and Cuba—our deep resolve to protect our security and our freedom against any form of aggression. We have also made clear our steadfast determination to limit the arms race. In three administrations, our soldiers and diplomats have worked together to this end, always supported by Great Britain. Prime Minister Macmillan joined with President Eisenhower in proposing a limited test ban in 1959, and again with me in 1961 and 1962.

But the achievement of this goal is not a victory for one side—it is a victory for mankind. It reflects no concessions either to or by the Soviet Union. It reflects simply our common recognition of the dangers in further testing.

This treaty is not the millennium. It will not resolve all conflicts, or cause the Communists to forego their ambitions, or eliminate the dangers of war. It will not reduce our need for arms or allies or programs of assistance to others. But it is an important first step—a step towards peace—a step towards reason—a step away from war.

Here is what this step can mean to you and to your children and your neighbors:

First, this treaty can be a step towards reduced world tension and broader areas of agreement. The Moscow talks have reached no agreement on any other subject, nor is this treaty conditioned on any other matter. Under Secretary Harriman made it clear that any nonaggression arrangements across the division in Europe would require full consultation with our allies and full attention to their interests. He also made clear our strong preference for a more comprehensive treaty banning all tests everywhere, and our ultimate hope for general and complete disarmament. The Soviet Government, however, is still unwilling to accept the inspection such goals require.

No one can predict with certainty, therefore, what further agreements, if any, can be built on the foundations of this one. They could include controls on preparations for surprise attack, or on numbers and type of armaments. There could be further limitations on the spread of nuclear weapons. The important point is that efforts to seek new agreements will go forward.

But the difficulty of predicting the next step is no reason to be reluctant about this step. Nuclear test ban negotiations have long been a symbol of East-West disagreement. If this treaty can also be a symbol—if it can symbolize the end of one era and the beginning of another—if both sides can by this treaty gain confidence and experience in peaceful collaboration—then this short and simple treaty may well become an historic mark in man's age-old pursuit of peace.

Western policies have long been designed to persuade the Soviet Union to renounce aggression, direct or indirect, so that their people and all people may live and let live in peace. The unlimited testing of new weapons of war cannot lead towards that end—but this treaty, if it can be followed by further progress, can clearly move in that direction.

I do not say that a world without aggression or threats of war would be an easy world. It will bring new problems, new challenges from the Communists, new dangers of relaxing our vigilance or of mistaking their intent.

But those dangers pale in comparison to those of the spiraling arms race and a collision course towards war. Since the beginning of history, war has been mankind's constant companion. It has been the rule, not the exception. Even a nation as young and as peace-loving as our own has fought through eight wars. And three times in the last two years and a half I have been required to report to you as President that this Nation and the Soviet Union stood on the verge of direct military confrontation—in Laos, in Berlin, and in Cuba.

A war today or tomorrow, if it led to nuclear war, would not be like any war in history. A full-scale nuclear exchange, lasting less than 60 minutes, with the weapons now in existence, could wipe out more than 300 million Americans, Europeans, and Russians, as well as untold numbers elsewhere. And the survivors, as Chairman Khrushchev warned the Communist Chinese, "the survivors would envy the dead." For they would inherit a world so devastated by explosions and poison and fire that today we cannot even conceive of its horrors. So let us try to turn the world away from war. Let us make the most of this opportunity, and every opportunity, to reduce tension, to slow down the perilous nuclear arms race, and to check the world's slide toward final annihilation.

Second, this treaty can be a step towards freeing the world from the fears and dangers of radioactive fallout. Our own atmospheric tests last year were conducted under conditions which restricted such fallout to an absolute minimum. But over the years the number and the yield of weapons tested have rapidly increased and so have the radioactive hazards from such testing. Continued unrestricted testing by the nuclear powers, joined in time by other nations which may be less adept in limiting pollution, will increasingly contaminate the air that all of us must breathe.

Even then, the number of children and grandchildren with cancer in their bones, with leukemia in their blood, or with poison in their lungs might seem statistically small to some, in comparison with natural health hazards. But this is not a natural health hazard — and it is not a statistical issue. The loss of even one human life, or the malformation of even one baby — who may be born long after we are gone — should be of concern to us all. Our children and grandchildren are not merely statistics toward which we can be indifferent.

Nor does this affect the nuclear powers alone. These tests befoul the air of all men and all nations, the committed and the uncommitted alike, without their knowledge and without their consent. That is why the continuation of atmospheric testing causes so many countries to regard all nuclear powers as equally evil; and we can hope that its prevention will enable those countries to see the world more clearly, while enabling all the world to breathe more easily.

Third, this treaty can be a step toward preventing the spread of nuclear weapons to nations not now possessing them. During the next several years, in addition to the four current nuclear powers, a small but significant number of nations will have the intellectual, physical, and financial resources to produce both nuclear weapons and the means of delivering them. In time, it is estimated, many other nations will have either this capacity or other ways of obtaining nuclear warheads, even as missiles can be commercially purchased today.

I ask you to stop and think for a moment what it would mean to have nuclear weapons in so many hands, in the hands of countries large and small, stable and unstable, responsible and irresponsible, scattered throughout the world. There would be no rest for anyone then, no stability, no real security, and no chance of effective disarmament. There would only be the increased chance of accidental war, and an increased necessity for the great powers to involve themselves in what otherwise would be local conflicts.

If only one thermonuclear bomb were to be dropped on any American, Russian, or any other city, whether it was launched by accident or design, by a madman or by an enemy, by a large nation or by a small, from any corner of the world, that one bomb could release more destructive power on the inhabitants of that one helpless city than all the bombs dropped in the Second World War.

Neither the United States nor the Soviet Union nor the United Kingdom nor France can look forward to that day with equanimity. We have a great obligation, all four nuclear powers have a great obligation, to use whatever time remains to prevent the spread of nuclear weapons, to persuade other countries not to test, transfer, acquire, possess, or produce such weapons.

This treaty can be the opening wedge in that campaign. It provides that none of the parties will assist other nations to test in the forbidden environments. It opens the door for further agreements on the control of nuclear weapons, and it is open for all nations to sign, for it is in the interest of all nations, and already we have heard from a number of countries who wish to join with us promptly.

Fourth and finally, this treaty can limit the nuclear arms race in ways which, on balance, will strengthen our Nation's security far more than the continuation of unrestricted testing. For in today's world, a nation's security does not always increase as its arms increase, when its adversary is doing the same, and unlimited competition in the testing and development of new types of destructive nuclear weapons will not make the world safer for either side. Under this limited treaty, on the other hand, the testing of other nations could never be sufficient to offset the ability of our strategic forces to deter or survive a nuclear attack and to penetrate and destroy an aggressor's homeland.

We have, and under this treaty we will continue to have, the nuclear strength that we need. It is true that the Soviets have tested nuclear weapons of a yield higher than that which we thought to be necessary, but the hundred megaton bomb of which they spoke of years ago does not and will not change the balance of strategic power. The United States has chosen, deliberately, to concentrate on more mobile and more efficient weapons, with lower but entirely sufficient yield, and our security is, therefore, not impaired by the treaty I am discussing.

It is also true, as Mr. Khrushchev would agree, that nations cannot afford in these matters to rely simply on the good faith of their adversaries. We have not, therefore, overlooked the risk of secret violations. There is at present a possibility that deep in outer space, that hundreds and thousands and millions of miles away from the earth, illegal tests might go undetected. But we already have the capability to construct a system of observation that would make such tests almost impossible to conceal, and we can decide at any time whether such a system is needed in the light of the limited risk to us and the limited reward to others of violations attempted at that range. For any tests which might be conducted so far out in space, which cannot be conducted more easily and efficiently and legally underground, would necessarily be of such a magnitude that they would be extremely difficult to conceal. We can also employ new devices to check on the testing of smaller weapons in the lower atmosphere. Any violations, moreover, involves, along with the risk of detection, the end of the treaty and the worldwide consequences for the violator.

Secret violations are possible and secret preparations for a sudden withdrawal are possible, and thus our own vigilance and strength must be maintained, as we remain ready to withdraw and to resume all forms of testing, if we must. But it would be a mistake to assume that this treaty will be quickly broken. The gains of illegal testing are obviously slight compared to their cost, and the hazard of discovery, and the nations which have initialed and will sign this treaty prefer it, in my judgment, to unrestricted testing as a matter of their own self-interests for these nations, too, and all nations, have a stake in limiting the arms race, in holding the spread of nuclear weapons, and in breathing air that is not radioactive. While it may be theoretically possible to demonstrate the risks inherent in any treaty, and such risks in this treaty are small, the far greater risks to our security are the risks of unrestricted testing, the risk of a nuclear arms race, the risk of new nuclear powers, nuclear pollution, and nuclear war.

This limited test ban, in our most careful judgment, is safer by far for the United States than an unlimited nuclear arms race. For all these reasons, I am hopeful that this Nation will promptly approve the limited test ban treaty. There will, of course, be debate in the country and in the Senate. The Constitution wisely requires the advice and consent of the Senate to all treaties, and that consultation has already begun. All this is as it should be. A document which may mark an historic and constructive opportunity for the world deserves an historic and constructive debate.

It is my hope that all of you will take part in that debate, for this treaty is for all of us. It is particularly for our children and our grandchildren, and they have no lobby here in Washington. This debate will involve military, scientific, and political experts, but it must be not left to them alone. The right and the responsibility are yours.

If we are to open new doorways to peace, if we are to seize this rare opportunity for progress, if we are to be as bold and farsighted in our control of weapons as we have been in their invention, then let us now show all the world on this side of the wall and the other that a strong America also stands for peace. There is no cause for complacency.

We have learned in times past that the spirit of one moment or place can be gone in the next. We have been disappointed more than once, and we have no illusions now that there are shortcuts on the road to peace. At many points around the globe the Communists are continuing their efforts to exploit weakness and poverty. Their concentration of nuclear and conventional arms must still be deterred.

The familiar contest between choice and coercion, the familiar places of danger and conflict, are all still there, in Cuba, in Southeast Asia, in Berlin, and all around the globe, still requiring all the strength and the vigilance that we can muster. Nothing could more greatly damage our cause than if we and our allies were to believe that peace has already been achieved, and that our strength and unity were no longer required.

But now, for the first time in many years, the path of peace may be open. No one can be certain what the future will bring. No one can say whether the time has come for an easing of the struggle. But history and our own conscience will judge us harsher if we do not now make every effort to test our hopes by action, and this is the place to begin.

According to the ancient Chinese proverb, "A journey of a thousand miles must begin with a single step."

My fellow Americans, let us take that first step. Let us, if we can, step back from the shadows of war and seek out the way of peace. And if that journey is a thousand miles, or even more, let history record that we, in this land, at this time, took the first step.

Thank you and good night.

Postscript: First Steps Toward Recovery

The world and your community would be shattered by a nuclear war. Normal services would be disrupted; essential skills could be in short supply; equipment you had taken for granted might not be available. You would face the aftermath of a catastrophe, but if there had been previous planning, you need not face it alone.

Using community resources

As in the case of natural disasters, community action is by far the best way to do all that must be done to recover from a nuclear attack. Local governments have at hand many organized units, such as the police and fire departments, the county road commission, and the health department, whose survivors can serve as a hard core for organized recovery actions immediately after people can emerge from shelters. Government agencies, military units, and other organizations, such as construction companies and the repairmen of the public utilities, would help to repair damage and restore service as soon as possible—as they have in past natural disasters. But many more helpers would be needed. Wherever you might be, in a community or family shelter, your help would be needed. If your community is lucky and receives little fallout, you may be needed to help a neighborhood community.

The communities that are well organized and have planned their recovery actions would be able to return to tolerable living conditions in the shortest time. The first job in this would be to clean up pre-selected areas to make them safe for living outside of shelters. The initial action may well originate with organized units in community shelters—from the basement of the city hall, from a shelter at a school—or it could come from groups in several shelters working together. As groups, they would have more of the manpower, equipment, and communications needed to start the job.

Getting rid of fallout

The process of removing fallout particles from exposed surfaces and disposing of the particles in places where they cannot harm people is called radiological decontamination.

Paved areas could be decontaminated with fire hoses or street flushers, using high-pressure nozzles, and with motorized street sweepers. Roofs could be decontaminated with fire hoses. Unpaved areas could be decontaminated by scraping off or plowing under a thin top layer of soil. This could be done with large earth-moving equipment — such as motorized scrapers and motor graders — on large open areas, and with bulldozers, tractor scrapers, shovels, and wheelbarrows on smaller areas around houses and trees. Another method would be to cover a contaminated area with clean earth.

In decontaminating paved areas, crews could flush the particles into storm drains or into ditches, where the particles could be covered with clean earth or picked up and hauled to a dumping area. The scrapings from the unpaved areas could be dumped in a pile about 100 feet from occupied areas, or hauled away. The dumping area might be a gully, refuse area, or even a vacant lot roped off at a safe distance.

Since the most effective and rapid methods of decontamination would involve the use of crews and equipment working in large areas, the best places to start the decontamination are likely to be at schools, shopping centers, and downtown areas, and at parks and open fields where large equipment can operate.

It is vital that communities set aside in advance many rallying points where people can meet to start work after an attack. If you are in a home shelter and have a ratemeter, you should wait until the radiation level has fallen to a point where you can go out for about an hour without receiving more than a few roentgens. You could use this time to go to your local school, shopping area, or other designated gathering place and join with your neighbors in community decontamination efforts.

If you do not have a radiation instrument, stay in shelter until you are assured, by radio, by contact from local authorities, or by other means, that clean areas are established near you and that it is safe to proceed there.

In areas of heavy fallout where the first decontamination actions can be started, if well organized, within the second week after attack, there is relatively little danger from fallout particles getting on people doing cleanup work — especially if normal habits of personal cleanliness are maintained. The most likely articles of clothing to pick up fallout particles are shoes, so keep them brushed clean.

Fallout Protection: What to Know and Do About Nuclear Attack
Department of Defense, Office of Civil Defense, 1961

It Could Happen Here!, Veterans of Foreign Wars Post No. 3477, Athens, Ohio, no date.

Bibliography of Civil Defense Publications, 1950–1965

The following is a list of federal, state, regional, and local civil defense publications released between 1950 and approximately 1965. Note that unless otherwise indicated, government publications were published in Washington, D.C., by the U.S. Government Printing Office.

Birmingham-Jefferson County (Alabama) Civil Defense Corps. *When the Bomb Goes Off—Don't Be There!* 1955.
Chicago Civil Defense Corps. *Chicagoland Civil Defense Manual.* American Radio Publications, Inc., Peoria, Illinois, January 1952.
_____. *Should An A-Bomb Fall.* 1951.
Commonwealth of Massachusetts, Civil Defense Agency. *Protection from the Atomic Bomb.* 1950.
Denver Civil Defense Office, *Be Prepared!* No date.
_____. *Evacuation Map and Instructions.* No date.
_____. *Handbook for Civilians: Just in Case Atom Bombs Fall.* 1951.
Executive Office of the President, National Security Resources Board. *Survival Under Atomic Attack.* 1950.
Federal Civil Defense Administration. *Atomic Blast Creates Fire ... Are You Prepared?* 1951.
_____. *Before Disaster Strikes ... What to Do Now About Emergency Sanitation at Home.* August 1953.
_____. *Bert the Turtle Says Duck and Cover.* No date.
_____. *Between You and Disaster.* 1956.
_____. *Civil Defense Household First-Aid Kit.* 1954.
_____. *Corner Room Shelter.* 1953.
_____. *Emergency Action to Save Lives.* July 1951.
_____. *Facts About Fallout.* 1955.
_____. *Facts About the H Bomb ... That Could Save Your Life!* 1955.
_____. *Grandma's Pantry Belongs in Your Kitchen.* 1955.
_____. *Home Protection Exercises.* November 1953.
_____. *In Case of Attack!* 1951.
_____. *Six Steps to Survival.* 1955.
_____. *This Is Civil Defense.* May 1951.
_____. *3 Minutes of Your Time.* 1953.
_____. What About You and Civil Defense? No date.
_____. What You Can Do Now! No date.
_____. *What You Should Know About Radioactive Fallout.* 1958.
_____. *Women in Civil Defense.* June 1952.
Georgia Civil Defense Division, in cooperation with State Department of Education. *Civil Defense Manual for Georgia Schools.* September 1952.

Georgia Office of Civil Defense. *Georgia Women in Civil Defense*. No date.
Ground Observer Corps, U.S. Air Force. *One Call*. No date.
_____. *The Time for Air Defense Is Now*. 1953.
Guide for Civil Defense Action in the Washington Warning Area. 1959.
Joplin, Missouri, City of. *Community Shelter Plan*. No date.
Kansas Civil Defense Council. *6 Survival Secrets for Atomic Attack*. No date.
Maryland State Roads Commission. *A Guide to Family Survival*. No date.
Milwaukee City Civil Defense Administration. *Evacuation Guide for a Civil Defense Emergency*. No date.
_____. *Your Civil Defense Manual: A Handbook on Personal Survival*. American Radio Publications, Peoria, Illinois. No date.
Nashville-Davidson County Civil Defense. *Nashville-Davidson County Civil Defense Survival Plan*. No date.
National Security Resources Board, Civil Defense Office. *Survival Under Atomic Attack*. 1950.
New York City Office of Civil Defense. *New York City's Civil Defense Needs You*. No date.
New York City Metropolitan School Study Council. *Let's Face It*. No date.
New York State Civil Defense Commission. *You and the Atomic Bomb, Public Pamphlet #1*. 1950.
_____. *You and Civil Defense*. No date.
New York State Department of Health. *Guide for Self-Help and Neighbor Help for the Injured*. 1951.
_____. *"Operation Survival" and You*. 1953.
New York State Civil Defense Commission. *Civil Defense and the Schools*. 1953.
New York State Department of Health, on behalf of the New York State Civil Defense Commission. *Assisting at the Birth of a Baby After Enemy Attack If No Doctor Is Available*. 1954.
Niagara (New York) Frontier Civil Defense Offices. *If the Niagara Frontier Is Bombed*. No date.
Office of Civil and Defense Mobilization. Emergency Sanitation at Home. 1958.
_____. *Family Fallout Shelter*. 1959.
_____. *Individual and Family Survival Requirements*. November 1959.
_____. *School/Shelter: An Approach to Fallout Protection*. September 1959.
_____. *Ten for Survival*. 1960.
What You Should Know About the National Plan for Civil Defense and Defense Mobilization. December 1958.
Office of Civil Defense, Department of Defense. *Fallout Protection: What to Know and Do About Nuclear Attack*. December 1961.
Ohio Valley Civil Defense Authority. *Will to Survive*. 1956.
Oregon State Civil Defense Agency. *Civil Defense in Oregon Schools: A Planning and Instruction Guide*. 1958.
Pennsylvania State Council of Civil Defense. *Civil Defense for Schools*. 1952.
Portland (Oregon) Disaster Relief and Civil Defense. *What to Do ... You and the Atomic Bomb*. 1950.
Portland (Oregon) Office of Civil Defense. *Your Guide for Defense Against the H-Bomb*. July 1955.
Portland (Oregon) Target Area Coordinating Council. *Survival Is Up to You!* 1960.
Sacramento (Calif.) Area Civil Defense Office, California Disaster Office, and Federal Office of Civil Defense. *"...And the Grasshopper Laughed and Played Until the Fall Came."* No date.
St. Paul (Minnesota) Civil Defense. *If We Are Bombed: A Handbook for Your Protection*. No date.
San Francisco Disaster Council and Corps. *It's Your Life ... The San Francisco Plan*. No date.
Silver Bow County and City of Butte (Montana) Civil Defense. *Evacuation Map*. No date.
Tacoma (Washington) Office of Civil Defense. *If You Are Bombed*. No date.
U.S. Army Medical Department. *What You Should Know About the Atomic Bomb*. 1950.
U.S. Department of Agriculture. *Radioactive Fallout on the Farm*. 1958.
_____. *Your Family Survival Plan*. May 1963.
U.S. Department of Commerce. *A Preliminary Report on Highway Needs for Civil Defense*. Bureau of Public Roads. October 1956.
U.S. Department of the Air Force. *Aircraft Recognition for the Ground Observer*. April 1955.
Veterans of Foreign Wars Post No. 3477, Athens, Ohio. *It Could Happen Here!* No date.

Index

Air Defense Command, U.S. Air Force 85
Air Defense Control Centers 89, 92
Air Defense Filter Center 91–93
air raid warning signal 96, 121–122, 138, 184, 186, 188, 192–193; *see also* evacuation signal; take cover signal
Aircraft Spotter Clubs 93
aircraft spotters 92; *see also* plane spotters
American National Red Cross 111
animals, farm 46–49
USS *Apogon* 22
USS *Arkansas* 22
Assisting at the Birth of a Baby After Enemy Attack If No Doctor Is Available 53–54
Atomic Energy Commission 39
atomics 119, 129
"Atoms for Peace" 199–205

B-29 Superfortress 1, 7
Baruch, Bernard 206
Be Prepared! 113–115
Berlin 207–298, 211
Bermuda Conference, 199
Bikini Islands (Atoll) 3, 19–24, 125
Birmingham-Jefferson County (Alabama) Civil Defense Corps 192
Boy Scouts 121
British "Grand Slam" bomb *see* "Grand Slam" bomb
By, For and About Women in Civil Defense 61–64

Capp, Al 77
Carleton, Dan 65
Central Intelligence Agency 76
China 206; *see also* Red China
Churchill, Winston 14
Civil Defense Agency of the Commonwealth of Massachusetts 5, 86–87
Civil Defense for Schools 118–128

Civil Defense in Oregon Schools 134–139
Civil Defense Manual for Georgia Schools 92–93, 129–133
Civil Defense Office of Denver 100
Clay, Lucius D. 94
CONELRAD 41, 83–85, 139, 153, 160, 177, 185, 188, 193
Continental Air Command 88
Cousins, Norman 1
Cuba 207–208, 211

Daughters of the American Revolution 61
decontamination 43–44, 46–49, 140
Denver Civil Defense Program 113

Eisenhower, Dwight D. 3, 4, 39, 105, 111, 171, 199–205
Emergency Medical Services of Civil Defense 69
Emergency Sanitation at Home 162–163
Evacuation Guide for a Civil Defense Emergency 175–176
evacuation signal 184, 186, 188, 193

Facts About Fallout 45
Facts About the H Bomb 105–107
USS *Falcon* 22
Fallout Protection: What to Know and Do About Nuclear Attack 150, 213
fallout shelters 150, 153–157, 158, 165–166, 178, 180
The Family Fallout Shelter 153–157
farms 46–49
Federal Civil Defense Act of 1950 2
Federal Civil Defense Administration 2, 39, 45, 55, 61–62, 75–77, 80, 83, 105–106, 111, 158, 171

Fels Plantarium, the Franklin Institute 3, 16
filter center *see* Air Defense Filter Center
4 Wheels to Survival 191

Georgia Office of Civil Defense 92–93, 129
Gimbel Broadcasting System 16
Girl Scouts 121
Goff, Aaron 119
Graebner, William 1
"Grand Slam" bomb 13
Grandma's Pantry 61–64
Ground Observer Corps 3, 88–91, 92–93
ground zero 1, 13, 69, 164

Hammarskjold, Dag 199
Harriman, William Averell 208
Harris, Innis D. 4, 76
Harris, Norman 123
USS *Haven* 21
Hirohito, Emperor 1
Hiroshima 1–3, 8, 12–15, 105, 108
Hoegh, Leo A. 3, 147
Home Defense Corps 2, 65–68
home defense pledge 75
Home Protection Exercises 158–161, 170
Hopalong Cassidy 123
USS *Hughes* 22

identification tags 2, 58, 183
If the Niagara Frontier Is Bombed 94–99
If We Are Bombed: A Handbook for Protection 74, 167
In Case of Attack! 83–85
Individual and Family Survival Requirements 147–149
Industrial College of the Armed Forces 4, 76
It Could Happen Here! 60, 198, 214

Index

Japanese fishermen 39, 41
Joint Chiefs of Staff 76; Evaluation Board 19
Joint Task Force One *see* Operations Crossroads
Junior Red Cross 121
Just in Case Atom Bombs Fall 100–104

Kennedy, John F. 3–4, 206–211
Khrushchev, Nikita 209–210
Korea 123, 127; Korean War 77

Life Under a Cloud: American Anxiety About the Atom 3
Living Wonders 123
The Lone Ranger 123
Lovett, Robert 55

Maine Civil Defense Agency 61
Maine State Grocers Association 63
Marshall, Dr. Roy K. 3, 16–18
Medical Aides 2, 69–72
Micronesian Islands *see* Bikini Islands
Milwaukee Civil Defense Administration 65, 108–109, 175–176
"Mr. Civil Defense" 77
Mobilization Plan of 1937 76
morale activities 143

Nagasaki 1, 8, 108
Nashville-Davidson County Civil Defense Survival Plan 186–191
National Blood Program 111
National Defense Pattern 133
National Interstate and Defense Highways Act of 1956 4, 171
The National Plan 182–183
National Policy on Shelters 3, 147–149
National Security Act of 1947 1, 76
National Security Council 76, 78
National Security Resources Board 77; Civil Defense Office 1, 33
New York State Civil Defense Commission 25, 53, 69, 71, 146
New York State Department of Health 53
Niagara Frontier Civil Defense Office 94

Oak Ridge, Tennessee 14
Office of Civil and Defense Mobilization 3, 140, 147, 153, 163–164, 182–183
Office of Defense Mobilization 77–80; *see also* Office of Civil and Defense Mobilization
Ohio Valley Civil Defense Authority 177
One Call: The Ground Observer Corps 88–91
Operation Alert 4, 76–82
Operation Crossroads 19–24, 27
Operation Ivy 105
Operation SKYWATCH 88
"Operation Survival" and You 69–72
Oregon State Civil Defense Agency 134

Partial Test Ban Treaty 3, 206–211
Pearl Harbor 1, 13, 76
Pennsylvania State Council of Civil Defense 118–119
plane spotters 3, 89, 92–93
Portland (Oregon) Target Area Coordinating Council 181
Postdam 14
Protection from the Atomic Bomb 5, 86–87

Radioactive Fallout on the Farm 46–49
Red China 127
Richland, Washington 14
Roosevelt, Franklin D. 14
Russia 7, 57, 127, 181; *see also* Soviet Union

St. Paul (Minnesota) Civil Defense 74, 167
USS *Saratoga* 22
Saturday Review of Literature 1
School/Shelter: An Approach to Fallout Protection 140–143
shelter supplies 151–152, 162–163
Southeast Asia 211
Soviet Union 1–4, 19, 25, 39, 83, 88. 90, 105, 192, 199, 201, 203–204, 206–211
Survival Is Up to You! 181–185
Survival Under Atomic Attack 30, 33–37

take cover signal 186, 193, 195
Ten for Survival: Survive Nuclear Attack 164–166
3 Minutes of Your Time Can Save a Life 111–112
Time (magazine) 1
The Time for Civil Defense Is Now! 91
Truman, Harry S 1–2, 7, 13–15, 16, 83

U-235 uranium 17
United Nations 3, 127, 199, 206
U.S. Bureau of Public Roads 171, 173
U.S. Department of Agriculture 46
U.S. Department of Defense 76, 111; Office of Civil Defense 150, 213
U.S. Department of Health, Education, and Welfare 80
U.S. Department of Labor 80

V-1/V-2 rockets 13
Vandenberg, Hoyt 8, 56
Veterans of Foreign Wars (Athens, Ohio) 198, 214
Veterans of Foreign Wars Auxiliary 61

weapons of mass destruction 4, 76
What You Can Do Now! 75
What You Should Know About Radioactive Fallout 39–44
When the Bomb Goes Off—Don't Be There! 192–195
Whitehead, Ennis 88
Will to Survive 177–180
Wing, Inez 1
Winkler, Allan 3
WIP Radio, Philadelphia 3, 16
Women in Civil Defense 55–59

You and Civil Defense 146
You and the Atomic Bomb: What to Do in Case of an Atomic Attack 25–29
Your Civil Defense Manual: A Handbook on Personal Survival 32, 38, 65–68, 108–110

Zoo Parade 123